Business
Studies
Complete Revision and Practice

Paul Clark

Published by BBC Active, an imprint of Educational Publishers LLP, part of the Pearson Education Group Edinburgh Gate, Harlow, Essex CM20 2JE, England

Text Copyright © Paul Clark 2002, 2010

Design and Concept Copyright © BBC Active 2008, 2010

Designed by specialist publishing services ltd

BBC logo © BBC 1996. BBC and BBC Active are trademarks of the British Broadcasting Corporation.

The right of Paul Clark to be identified as author of this Work has been asserted by him in accordance with the Copyright, Designs and Patents Act, 1988.

ISBN 978-1-4066-5437-0

Printed in China CTPSC/01

The Publisher's policy is to use paper manufactured from sustainable forests.

First published 2002

This edition 2010

Acknowledgement
The author would like to thank Jamie Staddon of Kingsley High School for his help in editing this edition.

The publishers are grateful to The Co-operative Group for permission to use the website extract on p.75.

Image acknowledgements
All photos used under licence from Shutterstock.com. Individual images © 2009 to artist or photographer as follows: p.5 Marcin Balcerzak, p.13 Elena Elisseeva, p.40 Zsolt Nyulaszi.

Minimum recommended system requirements
PC: Windows(r), XP sp2, Pentium 4 1 GHz processor (2 GHz for Vista), 512 MB of RAM (1 GB for Windows Vista), 1 GB of free hard disk space, CD-ROM drive 16x, 16 bit colour monitor set at 1024 x 768 pixels resolution
MAC: Mac OS X 10.3.9 or higher, G4 processor at 1 GHz or faster, 512 MB RAM, 1 GB free space (or 10% of drive capacity, whichever is higher), Microsoft Internet Explorer® 6.1 SP2 or Macintosh Safari™ 1.3, Adobe Flash® Player 9 or higher, Adobe Reader® 7 or higher, Headphones recommended

If you experiencing difficulty in launching the enclosed CD-ROM, or in accessing content, please review the following notes:
1 Ensure your computer meets the minimum requirements. Faster machines will improve performance.
2 If the CD does not automatically open, Windows users should open 'My Computer', double-click on the CD icon, then the file named 'launcher.exe'. Macintosh users should double-click on the CD icon, then 'launcher.osx'
Please note: the eDesktop Revision Planner is provided as-is and cannot be supported.
For other technical support, visit the following address for articles which may help resolve your issues:
http://centraal.uk.knowledgebox.com/kbase/

If you cannot find information which helps you to resolve your particular issue, please email: Digital Support@pearson.com.
Please include the following information in your ma
- Your name and daytime telephone number.
- ISBN of the product (found on the packaging.)
- Details of the problem you are experiencing - e.g.
- Details of your computer (operating system, RAM,

Contents

People in business

Business and marketing

Business environment

* Only available in the CD-ROM version of the book.

Exam board specification map

Topic coverage

AQA

Unit 1 Setting up a business	Unit 2 Growing as a business	Unit 3 Investigating business (Controlled assessment on content of Units 1 and 2)
• Starting a business: ideas, reasons, franchises • Aims/Objectives • Business Planning • Type of business structure • Location • Marketing: research, marketing mix for small business • Finance: sources of finance and support, using cash flow statements • People in business: recruitment, motivation, legal protection • Operations management: job/batch production, efficiency and technology, customer service and ICT	• Expanding a business: methods of growth, possible stakeholder conflict • Aims/Objectives • Business Planning • Type of company structure • Location • Marketing: marketing mix for large business, product life cycle • Finance: sources of finance for large business, using profit/loss and balance sheets • People in business: organisation charts and structures, recruitment, motivation, • Operations management: flow production, efficiency and quality assurance, internal and external growth	

Edexcel

Unit 1 Introduction to small business	Unit 2 Investigating small business (Controlled assessment on content of Unit 1)	Unit 3 Building a business
• Understanding customer needs/satisfaction • Market mapping • Analysing competitors • Adding value • Start-ups and franchises • Nature of enterprise; taking calculated risks, thinking creatively, innovating, planning ahead • Business objectives • Costs, revenue, profit • Cash flow forecasts • Start-up finance • Marketing mix • Limited liability • Keeping records, paying tax • Recruiting staff • Economic context: supply and demand, impact of interest rates, exchange rates and business cycle • Effect of business decisions on stakeholders		• Marketing and market research • Product life cycle • Branding and marketing mix • Design and research • Managing stock control and costs • Good customer service • Effective financial management: cash-flow changes, break-even, financing growth • People management: organisation, motivation, communication and rewards • The wider world; business ethics, environmental issues, international trade

OCR

Unit 1 Marketing and enterprise	Unit 2 Business and people	Unit 3 Production, finance and external environment
• Market research, marketing mix, ethical issues, franchising, e-commerce • Enterprise, role of entrepreneur, government support for business • Importance of business plan (Controlled assessment on content of Unit 1)	• Structure of business activity • Meeting needs of stakeholders, aims/objectives, different sectors, business interdependence • Business ownership and trade • Types of business ownership, integration and growth, location • Business workforce: recruitment, selection, training, motivation, laws, unions • Organisation and communication • Internal organisation, functional areas, work patterns, ICT and communications	• Production methods, job, batch, flow, adding value, improving efficiency • Production costs, different kinds of costs, economies of scale, break-even • Sources of finance, forecasting with cash-flow, • Profit/loss data • External influences: • Competitive environment; competition, monopoly and role of government • Business responsibility to environment, sustainability and ethics • Role of Government and tax, interest rates, consumer spending and population changes • Impact of trade, exchange rates and globalisation

Introduction

How to use GCSE Bitesize Complete Revision and Practice

Begin with the CD-ROM. There are five easy steps to using the CD-ROM – and to creating your own personal revision programme. Follow these steps and you'll be fully prepared for the exam without wasting time on areas you already know.

Topic checker

Step 1: Check

The Topic checker will help you figure out what you know – and what you need to revise.

Revision planner

Step 2: Plan

When you know which topics you need to revise, enter them into the handy Revision planner. You'll get a daily reminder to make sure you're on track.

Step 3: Revise

From the Topic checker, you can go straight to the topic pages that contain all the facts you need to know.

- Give yourself the edge with the Web*Bite* buttons. These link directly to the relevant section on the BBC Bitesize Revision website.

- Audio*Bite* buttons let you listen to more about the topic to boost your knowledge even further. *

Step 4: Practise

Check your understanding by answering the Practice questions. Click on each question to see the correct answer.

Exam Bite

Step 5: Exam

Are you ready for the exam? Exam*Bite* buttons take you to an exam question on the topics you've just revised. *

* Not all subjects contain these features, depending on their exam requirements.

Interactive book

You can choose to go through every topic from beginning to end by clicking on the Interactive book and selecting topics on the Contents page.

Exam questions

Find all of the exam questions in one place by clicking on the Exam questions tab.

Last-minute learner

The Last-minute learner gives you the most important facts in a few pages for that final revision session.

You can access the information on these pages at any time from the link on the Topic checker or by clicking on the Help button. You can also do the Tutorial which provides step-by-step instructions on how to use the CD-ROM and gives you an overview of all the features available. You can find the Tutorial on the Home page when you click on the Home button.

Other features include:

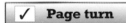

Click on the draw tool to annotate pages. N.B. Annotations cannot be saved.

 ✓ **Page turn**

Click on Page turn to stop the pages turning over like a book.

Click on the Single page icon to see a single page.

Click on this arrow to go back to the previous screen.

Contents

Click on Contents while in the Interactive book to see a contents list in a pop-up window.

Click on these arrows to go backward or forward one page at a time.

Click on this bar to switch the buttons to the opposite side of the screen.

Click on any section of the text on a topic page to zoom in for a closer look.

N.B. You may come across some exercises that you can't do on-screen, such as circling or underlining, in these cases you should use the printed book.

About this book

Use this book whenever you prefer to work away from your computer. It consists of two main parts:

 A set of double-page spreads, covering the essential topics for revision from each area of the curriculum. Each topic is organised in the following way:

- a summary of the main points and an introduction to the topic

- lettered section boxes cover the important areas within each topic

- key facts highlighting the essential information in a section or providing tips on answering exam questions

- practice questions at the end of each topic to check your understanding.

 A number of special sections to help you consolidate your revision and get a feel for how exam questions are structured and marked. These extra sections will help you to check your progress and be confident that you know your stuff.
They include:

- exam-style questions and worked model answers and comments to help you get full marks

- Topic checker – quick questions covering all topic areas

- Complete the facts – check that you have the most important ideas at your fingertips

- Last-minute learner – the most important facts in just a few pages.

About your exam

Get organised
You need to know when your exams are before you make your revision plan. Check the dates, times and locations of your exams with your teacher, tutor or school office.

On the day
Aim to arrive in plenty of time, with everything you need: several pens, pencils and a ruler.

On your way, or while you're waiting, read through your Last-minute learner.

GCSE Business Studies exam questions

GCSE Business Studies students are required to complete two exam papers in addition to a controlled assessment task. This book will help prepare you for the content required for the exams. The exam papers will have some short questions, on particular topics, which require answers ranging from a single sentence to paragraphs (it will be clear how long your answer should be from the style of question and the space provided in the answer booklet). Other questions are based on case studies, with some source material to study (this material is often supplied in advance of the exam). These questions test your knowledge and understanding across the course, not in just one topic.

Case study questions are generally in two or three parts and the source material may include such things as photographs, drawings, newspaper articles, company information, tables or graphs. Typically, the first question will ask about your understanding of this data; for example, 'What do you understand by the term … ?' Later questions are likely to become more open-ended, which means that there could be a range of possible answers. You will be asked to evaluate or suggest solutions to business problems; there is usually more than one viewpoint on any problem. Make it clear, for example, if you are writing from the point of view of a manager, a worker or a customer.

The format of the exam depends upon the exam board you are using. It is possible that the two exams are split so that the first relates to small-scale business whilst the second refers to larger businesses (check with your teacher). This book covers the knowledge required for both exams. The first section of the book demonstrates the process of a business starting up and then growing in size. Some topics may be relevant to both small and large businesses and so could appear in either exam. The questions at the end of each section in this book have been devised to offer practice for both small- and large-scale businesses.

About your controlled assessment

The controlled assessment is also designed to assess your Business Studies knowledge and understanding. You will be presented with a task with resource material. You will have between four and ten hours to carry out additional research and gather any background information required. You can work with other students during the research stage, but any written answers to tasks will have to be your own. Your teacher will be able to offer support and guidance throughout this stage. You will then have a further two to six hours to write up your report in exam conditions.

If you gather research materials in a folder during the investigation stage, then you will be asked to hand in this folder. The folders will be available only during the writing hours and not in between any sessions. Data from the folder can be used as supporting appendices for a task.

Different exam boards have based the controlled assessment on different units of the course. For those where the assessment focuses on a business start-up, you might be asked to decide on the best kind of business to start up in a particular setting. You could base this on what you know and what you can find out from websites about your local area; it might link to a shopping centre and you would consider competing businesses, your likely customers, the kinds of products, costs and prices. You might be asked for a written report or a summary in the form of a PowerPoint presentation. You should be clear about the key points and be able to offer reasons as to why your decisions are good ones. You should include examples of data from your local research to back up your conclusions. Marks are awarded for good use of data, good planning and good analysis and evaluation. This means making meaningful links between your data, your explanations and your judgements.

Note that examples of controlled assessments are included in guidance from the websites of exam boards.

Topic checker

Go through these questions after you've revised a group of topics, putting a tick if you know the answer.

You can check your answers on pages xiv–xvii.

>> Business types and objectives

1	What is meant by a 'secondary sector' business?	☐
2	What are the qualities of a successful entrepreneur?	☐
3	What is a 'sole trader'?	☐
4	How many partners can there be in a partnership?	☐
5	What is a 'deed of partnership'?	☐
6	What does 'limited liability' mean?	☐
7	What is the major difference between a 'Ltd' and a 'PLC'?	☐
8	What is a 'co-operative'?	☐
9	Why is a franchise often a good way of starting up in business?	☐
10	What are the main reasons for privatising a public sector organisation?	☐
11	What is meant by 'chain of command' in a business organisation?	☐
12	What is meant by 'span of control' in a business organisation?	☐
13	What is the name of the department which looks after the people in a business?	☐
14	Identify a business objective apart from making a profit.	☐
15	Who are the 'stakeholders' in a business?	☐

>> Business production

16	What is meant by 'customer-led' production?	☐
17	Why is a wide product range important?	☐
18	What are 'economies of scale'?	☐
19	What is the difference between batch and flow production methods?	☐
20	How can teamwork improve job satisfaction?	☐

21	What is the major benefit of 'just-in-time' production?	☐
22	What is meant by an increase in 'productivity'?	☐
23	What is meant by 'automation'?	☐
24	What is 'CAD'?	☐
25	Why is research and development important for quality control?	☐
26	What is 'total quality management' (TQM)?	☐
27	Why might a sawmill be likely to locate near a forest?	☐
28	Why is a small shop likely to locate away from a big shopping mall?	☐
29	How can a government encourage a business to move to a greenfield site?	☐
30	Why might a government stop a business moving to a particular site?	☐

>> Business finance

31	Why is financial planning important to a business?	☐
32	What is meant by an 'internal source' of finance?	☐
33	Why is a bank loan usually preferred to a bank overdraft?	☐
34	What is 'trade credit'?	☐
35	What are 'running costs'?	☐
36	What are 'expansion costs'?	☐
37	What is a 'business plan'?	☐
38	What is meant by a 'break-even' point for a business?	☐
39	What is the difference between fixed and variable costs?	☐
40	What is meant by 'margin of safety' when talking about production levels?	☐
41	What is a 'cash flow forecast'?	☐
42	Why is a profit and loss account important?	☐
43	What does a balance sheet show?	☐
44	What is meant by the 'working capital' of a business?	☐
45	Why is an acid test ratio important?	☐

Topic checker

>> People in business

46	Why is 'Maslow's hierarchy' important to personnel managers?	☐
47	Apart from money, what is a major reason for going to work?	☐
48	What is meant by a non-financial incentive to work hard?	☐
49	What is meant by 'performance-related pay'?	☐
50	Why are job descriptions important to employers and employees?	☐
51	What is 'induction training'?	☐
52	What is 'off-the-job training'?	☐
53	Why are government training schemes important?	☐
54	Why are good external communications important to a business?	☐
55	Why are written communications important within a business?	☐
56	Why is email important in a large company?	☐
57	What is meant by 'industrial relations'?	☐
58	What are trade unions?	☐
59	Why are health and safety laws important to business?	☐
60	What is 'collective bargaining'?	☐

>> Business and marketing

61	What is the importance of a SWOT analysis to a business?	☐
62	What is meant by a 'market segment'?	☐
63	What is the difference between primary and secondary data used in market research?	☐
64	What is a survey based on quotas?	☐
65	What are the 'four Ps' of the marketing mix?	☐
66	Why will the marketing mix vary from business to business?	☐
67	What is the major advantage and disadvantage of advertising via national TV networks?	☐
68	What is meant by a 'product life cycle'?	☐

69	Why is the product life cycle for a computer game different to that of a product like salt?	
70	Name one way in which the life cycle of a product can be extended.	
71	What is the major advantage of branding to a company?	
72	What is likely to happen to the price of a product if demand is greater than supply?	
73	What is meant by 'skimming' as a pricing policy?	
74	What is meant by 'direct mailing' as part of the promotion of a product?	
75	Why is packaging seen by some businesses as adding value to a product?	

>> The business environment

76	Identify three external influences affecting businesses.	
77	Give two reasons why competition is good for business.	
78	Give two examples of how the government protects consumers.	
79	What is the role of the Competition Commission?	
80	Give three examples of how a business can be ethically responsible.	
81	Give two examples of the external benefits of a business locating in an area.	
82	Give two examples of government policy which affect businesses.	
83	What is 'income tax'?	
84	What is 'value added tax' and who pays it?	
85	What is the 'European Union'?	
86	Identify three benefits of EU membership.	
87	What is the 'euro'?	
88	What is meant by 'global trade'?	
89	What is the meaning of 'the £ has gone up against the $'?	
90	What are 'tariffs'?	

Topic checker answers

>> Business types and objectives

1	Businesses using raw materials to produce finished goods
2	A person willing to take risks, be creative, show leadership, be organised
3	A business owned and controlled by one person
4	Between two and twenty
5	A set of rules to ensure good behaviour between partners
6	Owners are liable only for the money they have invested in the business.
7	Shares in a Ltd company are only available to original founders and their friends, not to the general public.
8	A business run for the benefit of the stakeholders, with each person having an equal share in it
9	The risks are minimised because the franchiser supports the franchisee as the business sets up.
10	To bring more competition and private finance into the business
11	The line of command from top to bottom in a business
12	The amount of responsibility of any particular person in a business
13	Human Resource department
14	To provide a service; to be charitable
15	People who have an interest in the business: includes managers, owners, customers, workers, local and national communities

>> Business production

16	Production where customer preferences determine what is made
17	It spreads the risk of failure when a product doesn't sell.
18	Cost savings which come from making the product on a large scale
19	Batch production uses large-scale processes to make a batch of one item before switching to another item; flow is a continuous production of identical items.
20	Workers are more involved with production decisions as they work together.
21	It cuts the costs of storing unnecessary stock levels.
22	An increase in the amount produced by each worker
23	Production is done completely by machine.
24	Computer-aided design, typically used where design models are important
25	Reseach and development can generate new ideas or new ways of producing goods to high quality.

26	Everyone is involved in quality management from the beginning to the end of the process.
27	Because the wood is nearby, it can be cut down to size immediately, making it easier to transport to market.
28	Because rates and other costs are very high in big shopping centres
29	By offering grants to businesses which move
30	Because the business might spoil an area of beauty or bring pollution

>> Business finance

31	It helps to keep costs under control and allows for unexpected events.
32	Finance found from within the business, usually from retained profits
33	Because rates of interest are usually lower on loans
34	Where goods bought are paid for at a later date
35	The regular costs of producing goods or services, e.g. wages
36	The costs of expanding a business, such as buying a new factory or machinery
37	A plan of the predicted performance of a business, usually prepared for a lender
38	The point at which the costs of production are just met by sales revenue
39	Variable costs change with the amount of customers or sales; fixed costs don't.
40	The amount of spare money available because revenue is greater than costs
41	A prediction of the cash flowing in and out of the business over a specified period
42	Provides managers and others with a record of all the revenue and costs during the last accounting period (usually a year)
43	A snapshot showing all the assets and liabilities of a business
44	The finance immediately available for running the business (current assets minus current liabilities)
45	It shows how easily a business could cover its short-term debts.

>> People in business

46	It provides a guide for motivating people: take care of basic needs first and then think about job satisfaction and higher needs.
47	Because many people see work as a source of personal satisfaction and self-esteem
48	Things like praise and the opportunity for promotion which makes a person try harder
49	Pay is linked to the achievement of agreed targets.

50	Because they clarify exactly what is expected of a person in any job
51	Training to help new employees settle into a workplace
52	Training which takes place away from the workplace
53	Because they provide support for employees to help them move jobs or to retrain with new skills – businesses cannot always afford to pay for such training
54	These are the links between a business and its customers or its suppliers; customers will not buy the products of a business which treats them badly.
55	They provide a permanent record of communications; especially important when the issues are the subject of disagreement.
56	It helps to speed up communication between employees and saves time and money.
57	The relationship between the workforce and the management of a business
58	Organisations that look after the interests of workers in a particular 'trade' or kind of business
59	They make sure every business has proper health and safety procedures in place; they set standards for every business.
60	A process of negotiation which involves every side with an interest in the result

>> Business and marketing

61	It provides a breakdown of the strengths and weaknesses of the business and of opportunities to expand in the future.
62	A division of a business's potential market based on their different characteristics, e.g. sex, age, location, income and lifestyle
63	Primary data is collected first hand; secondary data is collected and published by someone else.
64	Where data is collected from a pre-determined set of people; the interviewer has to ask a given number of people from each market segment
65	Price, promotion, product, place
66	Because each business will have different needs, e.g. some may wish to compete mainly by price rather than through advertising
67	Reaches a national audience but can be expensive
68	The different stages of a product from initial development through to closure after loss of sales
69	A computer game sells for a limited period while it is in fashion; salt is always wanted for cooking and there is no obvious replacement for it.
70	By extra advertising; by widening the product range; by changing the product image
71	It distinguishes your product from that of rivals

72	The price will rise because consumers are keen to get hold of the product.
73	Charging high prices while a product is new and fashionable; the price is often then reduced to attract other consumers
74	Direct mailing means sending promotional leaflets directly to the homes of consumers or to business customers.
75	Packaging can 'add value' if the final product is seen to be worth more to the consumer.

>> The business environment

76	Business rivals; government; pressure groups
77	Helps to keep down costs; encourages new products
78	Passes laws like the Trade Descriptions Act; provides agencies like the Trading Standards Office
79	Investigates businesses which have a large share of any market to make sure they are behaving well
80	By considering the interests of the local community where the business is located, by selling fairly-traded goods, by reducing waste material in packaging of goods
81	Business employees bring extra spending into the community; the business may develop a local road to everyone's benefit
82	Policies which help to bring lower interest rates and so make borrowing cheaper; the government takes tax from businesses which can be used to help poorer people in the community
83	A tax taken from every worker's pay, linked to how much they earn; very low wages are not taxed at all
84	A tax on spending which covers most goods and services; everyone who buys the goods pays the tax
85	The European Union (EU) is a common trading area for member countries.
86	Easier trade between members as there are no taxes when crossing borders; a shared currency; consumer protection laws which apply across the EU
87	The common European currency which has replaced national currencies for most EU members
88	Taking part in trade across continents
89	The exchange rate of the £ has gone up compared with that of the US$; a customer with £s can now buy more US goods for the same money.
90	A tax on imports used by governments to protect their own businesses from foreign imports

Business types

 Businesses can be classified (grouped together) in different ways:
- **by sectors of activity or industrial groupings**
- **by the way they are financed and controlled**
- **by their different objectives.**

A Different types of business

Business types include sole traders, partnerships, companies and co-operatives.

>> **key fact** Different business types can be linked together in a chain of production.

1 John: **sole trader** on his own farm growing crops such as wheat (primary sector).

2 Rank Hovis MacDougall PLC: large food-manufacturing **company** (secondary sector) owned by shareholders. Aims to supply affordable bread through supermarkets nationwide and make profits for shareholders.

3 Co-op supermarkets: a wholesaling and retail service; gets bread and other products to customers at convenient sites. As a **co-operative**, customers and workers are part-owners and share the benefits.

4 Tom's bakery: supplies high-quality bread and cakes to customers in the local area. He and a friend run the business in **partnership**.

Customers

B Sectors of business activity

>> **key fact** To look at changes in business activity it is helpful to use three broad groupings called sectors.

1 **Primary sector**: extract raw materials from land or sea, e.g. mining.
- Britain was once highly dependent on this sector for income and jobs.

2 **Secondary sector**: use raw materials to make finished goods, e.g. car makers.
- Manufacturing has been hit by foreign competition.

3 **Tertiary sector**: provide a service to industry/consumers, e.g. retail.
- This is the fastest growing sector in Britain.

C Chain of production

>> **key fact** Businesses in one sector are linked to, and dependent on, those in other sectors. At each stage in the chain a business will try to add value.

A chain of production for the oil industry (as shown here) and for the bread industry (opposite) demonstrates the interdependence of businesses.

Oil extraction (primary) → Oil refining (secondary) – produces a range of products, e.g. petrol, plastics → Retail (tertiary), e.g. petrol stations

D Trends in UK

1968
- primary
- secondary
- tertiary

2008

UK output has changed throughout the last century. The graphs show that there has been a significant shift in the UK from the secondary sector towards the tertiary sector. Causes for this include:

- increased demand for financial services and other tertiary sector industries from UK

- manufacturing firms moved to Asia due to lower wages.

remember >>

As the UK specialises more in tertiary sector products, it has to trade more with other countries for manufactured goods.

E Chain of production

>> **key fact** Business activities can be classified into eight industrial groupings.

- The groupings are: agriculture, forestry, fishing; distribution, hotels, repairs; energy and water; transport and communication; manufacturing; construction; banking, finance, insurance; education and health.

- They can be used to examine changes in employment and production, and are widely used in government statistics.

>> practice questions

1 **Classify each of the following businesses as either primary, secondary or tertiary:**

a) a food manufacturer   b) a fishing company

c) a car repair centre   d) a private school.

2 **Services in the tertiary sector include advertising, banking and communication services.**

Explain how each of these services could support a business such as a car manufacturer.

Enterprise and business planning

- An entrepreneur is someone who takes on the risk of a new business venture.

- Entrepreneurs must plan their business in order to gain necessary finance at the start-up stage.

A The qualities of an entrepreneur

>> **key fact** An entrepreneur – the person who starts an enterprise – is a person who:
- is prepared to take calculated risks to start a new business
- is often creative and can see an opportunity to make and sell a new product
- shows determination and leadership
- can plan ahead.

B Choosing a product

>> **key fact** As part of starting a business, entrepreneurs must decide on the product to be made or the sevice to be provided.

They are likely to consider the following possibilities:

- develop a completely new product. This is often the result of using new technology

- improve or develop an existing product

- respond to new demands from consumers. Changing fashions, for example, create opportunities for new businesses.

C Looking for a gap in the market

>> **key fact** New products can be either product-driven or market-driven.

- A product-driven firm develops a product and then tries to market it to customers.

- A market-driven firm will identify what the market wants and then try to develop products to meet their wants and needs.

D Reasons for starting a business

Entrepreneurs choose to start their own business and take on the risk associated with it. Reasons for doing this may include a desire to:

- have the freedom to run the business their own way

- feel a sense of achievement if the business succeeds

- have the prospect of high earnings.

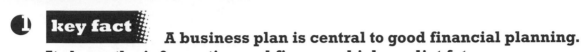

E Business plans

① key fact A business plan is central to good financial planning. It shows the information and figures which predict future performance of the business.

- A business plan plays a vital role in financial planning, especially if other organisations, such as banks, are to be asked for loans.

- It is a formal, detailed document, which explains how the finance for a business is going to be raised.

- It contains a cash flow and other financial forecasts.

- It shows how soon the business is likely to break even.

- It includes background information (e.g. product/service offered, number of staff, target market).

- It shows the targets being set (the business objectives).

remember >>

Finance involves risks for business owners and for lenders. Will the possible profit outweigh the risk?

② key fact A business plan provides different kinds of information for different stakeholders.

It helps managers:

- to avoid costly mistakes

- to set targets for review

- by providing financial guidelines.

It provides vital information for lenders:

- the clarity of the managers' planning

- the length of time it will probably take to repay the loan

- the risks of the business venture.

>> practice questions

1 A group of 18-year-olds ask you, a bank manager, for a £5000 loan to help start a mobile disco business. They hope to be in profit after a year. What information would you expect to see in their business plan? If you loaned the money, what rules would you make for repayment?

2 Why are market-driven firms frequently more successful than product-driven firms?

Business objectives

- Business objectives show what a business aims to achieve.

- A business's success can be measured in terms of meeting these targets.

- Different stakeholders may have different objectives for a business.

A Types of business objectives

>> **key fact** Businesses can pursue three broad objectives (or aims).

1. **To make a profit** – the key concern for most private businesses.

2. **To provide a service** – the objective for most public sector businesses (e.g. schools, hospitals). They usually aim to break even.

3. **To be charitable** – some businesses' sole aim is to help others. They operate as any efficient business and often have to compete for funds.

Business objectives can be found in company reports and publicity material.

These provide a statement of purpose for the business and are often referred to as a **mission statement**.

B More detailed objectives and targets

Within these general headings, businesses set themselves more detailed objectives. Examples of these, and ways they might be achieved, are shown below:

1. To **maximise profits**, by keeping costs as low as possible and by setting a price to bring in the most revenue (a chocolate firm charges a high price for their luxury chocolates)

2. To win a **larger share of the market**, by taking over a rival business (a French car company takes over a British firm to increase sales in the UK)

3. To ensure **long-term survival**, by borrowing money to invest in developing new products (an international airline borrows money to buy jets for long-haul flights)

4. To ensure **services reach those in most need**, by restricting them to a named group at a time (a hospital targets emergency treatment for elderly heart patients)

5. To **be ethical**, by supporting a particular cause such as the environment or animal welfare (a stationery business plants two trees to replace every one used in making the paper products).

Once established, these objectives are documented in fine detail, and targets are set (e.g. a certain increase in profit by a set date).

To be of use in measuring success, these targets must be **SMART**.

S pecific
M easurable
A ttainable
R ealistic
T imed

C Striking a balance

>> **key fact** Businesses need to strike a balance between their objectives.

Different businesses give their objectives different levels of importance.

1. The most important objective for many private businesses is profit, but not at any price. Some businesses are keen to maintain customer satisfaction and a reputation for quality.

2. Businesses may accept a drop in profits or sales to keep their independence.

3. Some objectives are measurable and short term, like profit; others are more general and long term, such as independence.

4. Public sector businesses aim to provide a good service, with high levels of customer satisfaction and efficient use of resources. However, they must also meet tight financial targets.

D Stakeholders' objectives

>> **key fact** Stakeholders are groups that have an interest in the success of a business.

Their objectives often vary:

remember >>

Stakeholders' objectives can overlap but may sometimes be conflicting.

Local community: local jobs, clean environment

Customers: value for money, choice

Suppliers: repeat orders, reliable payment of bills

Business

Owners: survival in business, best return on investment

Managers: best salary, status for department

Employees: job satisfaction, good pay

>> practice questions

Ragbags Ltd makes and sells children's clothes in the north of England. The managers want to increase sales in the south, by opening several new stores. But some of the business owners are worried that the new investment will affect profitability.

1 Why might the managers want to increase sales?

2 Why might some business owners be more interested in keeping profits high?

3 How might expansion affect customers?

4 How could the managers persuade owners to support the proposed expansion?

Business location

- A business chooses its location for many reasons, including economic and legal ones.

- The best location is often the result of a trade-off between different factors.

A Factors affecting business location

1 Labour
A business requiring a highly skilled workforce needs to be in an area linked to the industry or one with local training facilities.

A business looking for mainly unskilled, cheap labour looks for an area with a plentiful supply; low costs of transporting staff; and where staff can be persuaded to relocate.

2 Raw materials and the market
Firms dealing with perishable goods (e.g. canning and freezing firms) need to locate near to where the goods are produced.

Businesses whose process is bulk-reducing (e.g. brickmakers, a sawmill) locate near to the source of materials, to reduce transport costs.

Bulk-increasing businesses (e.g. car manufacturers) locate close to the market.

3 Land
The amount and cost of land will affect choice.

The nature of the land may be important (e.g. chemical plants need large, flat sites, which can bear heavy loads). A site in bad condition needs more investment.

Local planning restrictions must be considered.

5 Other influences
Climate.

Competition and/or co-operation with other businesses.

Government/pressure group influence.

Personal preferences of a business owner.

4 Infrastructure and services
All businesses need: good sources of energy and water; efficient drainage and waste disposal; good communications; fast, efficient transport links.

Locating to a remote, undeveloped site means paying to link up to such systems. Access to the Internet makes this less of an issue for some businesses.

remember >>

The reasons for location may be unique to a business or to its owner.

B Government and pressure groups

>> **key fact**　Government and private pressure groups can influence where a business locates.

The UK and European governments
- Financial support offered to businesses willing to move to areas of high unemployment.
- Twenty-four Enterprise Zones are examples of past policy in the UK.

Recent government policy
- Businesses encouraged to move to 'greenfield' sites (old farm or wasteland) or to 'brownfield' sites (derelict industrial areas in the heart of cities).
- New, purpose-built industrial estates have been created.

Business

Pressure groups
Groups representing a particular local, national or international interest may try to discourage development for environmental reasons (e.g. pollution, protection of habitats), or safety reasons (e.g. siting of toxic waste too close to human populations).

Government restrictions
The government can restrict land use or disallow it altogether due to, for example, the size of a proposed development, its negative impact on a local community, or the damage that will be done to a site of great beauty.

>> practice questions

1 Give three factors that a business should consider in locating an outdoor theme park.

2 Place in order of importance the factors that you have chosen. Explain the reasons for your chosen order.

exam tip >>

If you're asked to select the best location, it means you must compare the advantages and disadvantages of at least two different sites.

exam tip >>

There are no 'right' answers here but make sure the factors are relevant to an outdoor theme park.

Sole traders and partnerships

> **Businesses can be classified by how they are owned and financed, and on the basis of their legal responsibilities.**

> **A sole trader is a business owned and controlled by one person. Partnerships are owned by at least two partners.**

A Sole traders and partnerships

1 key fact Sole traders (sole proprietors) and partnerships are the smallest forms of business but are the easiest to set up.

- They make an important contribution to the economy, accounting for over 90% of UK businesses.

- They carry big risks of failure and of incurring debts for their owners, but they also allow individuals to turn an enterprising idea or skill into a business activity.

2 key fact A sole trader is a business owned and controlled by one person.

Sole traders operate under their own name and assume responsibility for the running of the business. They are the most common type of business in the UK.

3 key fact Partnerships are owned by the partners. There must be a minimum of two and usually a maximum of twenty partners.

- Responsibilities can be shared, with the business benefiting from the expertise of all the partners.

- There is less disruption when someone leaves the business as other partners remain to share their knowledge and keep contact with customers.

- Most partnerships write a **Deed of Partnership** – a set of rules to follow if trust between partners breaks down. A Deed usually covers the sharing of profits and losses, the **financial contribution** of each partner, their responsibilities, and how partners may be added to or removed from the business. Under the 1980 Partnership Act, everything is shared equally if there is no Deed or similar formal agreement.

> **remember >>**
>
> **Partnerships are common in professions like medicine and law where businesses are not allowed to limit their liability.**

1 Have unlimited liability, which means the owners are personally responsible for the debts of the business.

Sole traders and partnerships

3 Finance comes from their own resources, bank loans or government grants, if available.

2 Do not have to make public their business dealings.

B Setting up in business

Whether sole trader or partnership, the basics for setting up in business are:

- permission to trade in an area (a local council licence may be needed)

- registration to pay VAT (Value Added Tax) if turnover is above a certain level

- profit and loss accounts and a balance sheet so that the business can be assessed for tax and insurance contributions

- a knowledge of health and safety laws and a willingness to obey the rules.

C Advantages and disadvantages

Sole trader

✔ makes all the decisions, keeps all the profits, has total control, low start-up costs, business flexibility, job satisfaction

✖ unlimited liability (can lose personal wealth if business fails), lack of capital, pressure of responsibility

Partnership

✔ easy to set up, expertise available through partners, greater availability of finance, shared responsibilities mean less pressure

✖ liability still rests with partners, each partner is responsible for debts of others, disagreements possible

remember >>

Learn the pros and cons of different business types.

Case study

Three years ago, John Taylor opened a newsagency as a sole trader with the help of his wife. He had previously worked for a big supermarket but wanted a new challenge. It cost him £10000 to set up but he was left to work long hours when his wife fell ill. He employed an assistant manager but the shop began to lose money. The shelves were half empty and customers complained about a lack of choice. John decided to go into partnership with a friend.

>> practice questions

1 Using examples from the case study, or from your own knowledge, explain the meaning of:

a) unlimited liability

b) partnership.

2 a) Describe three advantages of being a sole trader.

b) What reasons might explain why a third of sole traders cease trading within their first year of operation?

exam tip >>

Use examples to help your explanation.

Growing a business

- An important objective for many businesses is to grow larger. They can sell more products in more places and aim to make more profit.

- There are two main ways in which businesses can grow: internally or externally.

A Internal growth

>> **key fact** Internal growth is through expanding an existing business.

A retail business could choose to expand an existing shop, open up additional shops in new locations or expand the product range.

This method of growth has been popular amongst UK supermarkets. They are selling a much wider range of 'non-food' items, they are opening new stores including different types of store such as town centre and local outlets, and they are expanding many of their existing buildings.

B External growth

>> **key fact** External growth is expanding through the process of a merger or take-over.

It is often a much quicker way for businesses to expand. A merger is when two separate businesses join together to form one entirely new organisation. A take-over describes the act of one business buying another outright.

There are different methods of external growth available to businesses.

1 **Horizontal** – this is where a business joins with another in the same industry and at the same stage of production. This enables the business to increase its market share and often benefit from cutting some costs.

2 **Vertical** – this is where a business joins with another in the same industry, but at a different stage of the production process. A vertical take-over could be forwards or backwards.

- A **forward take-over** involves one business buying another at a later stage in the production chain. This enables the business to ensure an outlet for its products and may restrict competitors' sales.

- A **backward take-over** involves a business buying another at an earlier stage in the production chain. This ensures high quality and punctual supply of products and may also restrict supplies to its competitors.

3 **Diversification** – this is where a business joins with another in an unrelated industry. It enables a business to spread its risks of failure and chances of success across a wide range of products.

C Stay small?

Some businesses will choose to remain small and not grow. There are also benefits associated with remaining small. Some niche markets are small and there is no need to produce on a large scale. Small businesses can often provide a more localised service and also offer a more personal touch which can boost image and popularity.

Case study

Stead's Smoothies manufacture luxury fruit drinks and the owners have been gradually expanding the business through a policy of internal growth. While pleased with the progress, they are frustrated by the time it is taking to grow. The owners have decided that they would like to take over another business in order to grow more rapidly.

>> practice questions

1   What kinds of business could Stead's Smoothies consider taking over? Provide an example for each type of external growth.

2   Which kind of growth would you recommend as best for the owners of Stead's and why?

exam tip >>

Assess advantages and disadvantages for each and then make your conclusion.

Ltd companies and PLCs

- There are two types of company – private limited (Ltd) and public limited (PLC). Both sell shares to raise finance. Limited refers to liability.

- Companies differ from sole traders/partnerships in how they are run and financed, and in the risks posed to the owners.

A Companies

1 key fact Companies are usually larger than partnerships/sole traders.

- They can be locally based with modest turnover or multinational giants with millions of shareholders and worldwide activities.

2 key fact There are two types of company – Ltds and PLCs.

- Shareholders own the company; they have a say in the running of the company and share in its profits by way of annual dividends.

- The company has its own legal identity, separate from that of the shareholders.

3 key fact 'Limited' in both cases refers to limited liability.

Share size decides how much profit shareholders gain, and also limits their risk of losses – they can only lose the money they invested in the business.

B Private limited company (Ltd)

> **key fact** A Ltd company is usually small- to medium-sized and sells shares privately to family and friends.

- The original owners, as the board of directors, keep control. Managers are often appointed to run the day-to-day business.

- Money raised by selling new shares helps finance business development.

> **remember >>**
>
> A company must satisfy customers and shareholders.

C Public limited company (PLC)

> **key fact** A PLC is usually large and sells shares to the public.

- Founders may lose control over decisions: shareholders appoint directors/managers.

- The interests of shareholders and managers can differ – the AGM and annual report help to keep everyone informed and involved.

- Banks and financial institutions are more prepared to finance PLCs.

D Setting up a company

>> key fact It is a similar process to set up both a Ltd company and a PLC, but there are more rules and regulations for a PLC.

- Company information is sent to the official registrar of companies, who grants a Certificate of Incorporation (the business gets its legal identity).

- Shares are sold and the company starts trading.

- A PLC needs at least £50 000 of finance and must produce a prospectus of financial detail for potential shareholders.

remember >>

PLCs are private companies, not state-run.

Limited liability
No one is personally liable for company debts.

Ltds and PLCs

Finance
From sale of shares, bank loans, government grants.

Requirements
AGM; annual report for shareholders; audited accounts sent to registrar of companies and open to public scrutiny.

Ltds	PLCs
shares sold only to founders, relatives and friends	shares listed on Stock Exchange, sold to public
at least 1 shareholder, 1 director, 1 secretary	at least 2 shareholders, 2 directors, qualified Company Secretary
takes time to sell shares; no minimum capital	shares sold easily; minimum share capital £50 000
founders of company retain control	original owners may have little influence on decisions
less status than PLC; loans more difficult	large organisation, high status, good credit rating
shareholders likely to agree on objectives	may be divisions between shareholders and managers

>> practice questions

Greens Ltd sells snacks to the public and catering trade.
Shares are owned by the Green family.

1 What do the letters Ltd stand for?

2 Identify two important features of a Ltd company.

3 The owners of Greens have limited liability. What does this mean?

4 Why might the Green family not want to turn the company into a PLC, despite needing the money that could be raised by issuing new shares?

Co-operatives and franchises

- **Co-operative:** run by people (producers, workers, consumers) with shared business interests, for the benefit of all involved.

- **Franchise:** small traders use a well-known company's trade name; the company benefits from the experience of local managers.

A Co-operatives

>> **key fact** Co-operatives are run by people with a shared business interest, to benefit all involved. Each participant has an equal say.

1) Workers' co-operatives

- Workers buy/set up a business then share decision-making and profits – this is the most common type of co-operative.

- Each worker invests an equal amount of money.

Advantages ✔	Disadvantages ✘
Close ties with local people	Expansion may be difficult – banks often reluctant to lend
Well-motivated workforce	Possible internal disputes over decisions and financial rewards
Fosters good industrial relations	Often lack business knowledge, but unwilling to buy managerial expertise

2) Producers' co-operatives

- Producers set up a marketing and retail operation, to reduce costs and prices.

- Often founded by farmers and wine producers. Expensive machinery can be bought and shared; products are sold directly to consumers.

3) Consumers' co-operatives

- Consumers set up an organisation to bulk-buy goods, then share the profits.

Case study

The best-known UK co-operative is the group which includes the Co-op Retail Society and the Co-op Bank. The retail movement, set up in Rochdale, Lancashire, in the 1840s, now has over 5000 shops and a turnover in excess of £8 million.

The Rochdale Co-op established principles which have guided other consumer co-ops:

- Each member has one vote.

- Anyone can buy a share.

- Goods/services are sold at a reasonable price with profits returned to members in proportion to the amount they spend.

B Franchises

>> **key fact** A franchise allows a trader to use a well-known company's trade name and enables the company to benefit from the experience of local managers.

1 The **franchisee** uses a trade name, image and even products in return for regular fees.

2 The **franchiser** can operate in many places using the experience of local managers.

3 In 2006, there were over 35 000 franchises in the UK. McDonald's, The Body Shop and Holiday Inn are some well-known examples.

4 Franchises have a better chance of establishing new businesses than sole traders, but disputes over day-to-day control can arise.

Franchiser's benefits includes	Franchisee's benefits includes
Business grows without risk of debt (franchisee responsible for debts)	Less risk during start-up
Regular income	Keep most of the profits (sometimes a percentage of income is paid to franchiser)
Less organisation and fewer staff than if a branch was opened	Selling established product and utilising successful brand image
Keep control (including choice of franchisee)	Allows for national marketing at less expense
Franchisees are usually highly-motivated with local knowledge	Assistance and training available

Case study

Mike and Alan enjoy skateboarding and are good at making boards. They decide to set up a business in a rented workshop. They pool their money and buy some materials. Unfortunately, neither relish the task of marketing and selling the boards. After six months, they have sold only a couple to friends, are still paying rent, and have no storage room left.

>> practice questions

1 Outline the potential advantages to Mike and Alan in buying a franchise from a national skateboarding company.

2 What extra costs would be incurred if Mike and Alan bought a franchise?

exam tip >>

Check carefully: is this about franchiser or franchisee?

The public sector

- Some organisations are so important to a nation that they are owned and controlled by the government.

- These public sector organisations are financed by taxes as well as by selling goods and services.

A Why public sector organisations exist

Governments run public sector organisations for a variety of reasons.

1. Security – some organisations are:
   - **vital to the defence** and stability of a nation (e.g. army, police force)
   - **'politically sensitive'** (e.g. arms research, disposal of nuclear waste).
2. Economic – **natural monopolies** where it makes sense to have one supplier (e.g. gas).
3. Financial – high levels of investment can put off private firms (e.g. train stations).
4. Social – some organisations provide **essential services** (e.g. education, health).
5. Organisational – co-ordinating agencies are often in the public sector. They:
   - **co-ordinate activities** of private businesses (e.g. Learning and Skills Councils)
   - **ensure businesses follow rules** to protect consumers (e.g. Trading Standards Authority).

B Is private or public best?

Reasons for privatisation	Reasons against privatisation
Better and quicker decision-making	Monopolies can charge high prices or cut services
Competition encourages efficiency	Non-profitable services may be cut
Need for government subsidies reduced	Competition can be wasteful as resources are duplicated
More people can be shareholders	Profits go to those who can afford shares
	May be a risk of job losses

C The story so far

1. In the UK, before 1979, over fifty large organisations (e.g. water, railways) were owned and run by the government. Co-ordinating one national network was thought to be more efficient than having competing businesses.

2. From 1979, successive governments have privatised many industries (e.g. BT, British Rail) – returning them to the private sector by selling shares to businesses and individuals. It was believed this increased efficiency, with government retaining some control via regulation.

3. Two more public sector organisations, the Royal Mail and London Underground, have partially privatised their activities.

(4) As some private banking and rail businesses ran into difficulties in 2008, the government took more control in regulating their activities. They are now effectively running as a mix of private and public sector businesses.

D Public and private sector mixes

>> **key fact** Most countries have public and private sector organisations. In the UK, these sectors work together in different ways.

(1) Internal markets

- In the health service and local councils, departments compete against each other, and often private companies, to win contracts.

- Schools have control over their own budgets and compete for pupils in local areas.

(2) Private finance

- The main services in schools, hospitals and for road maintenance are paid via taxes but if major new finance is needed, businesses can provide the money (and earn profits).

(3) Quangos

- Quasi Autonomous Non-Governmental Organisations (e.g. the British Tourist Board, National Parks) are partly independent but government-funded.

>> **key fact** Even without owning a business, governments can control business activity by making rules or supervising finances.

>> practice questions

1 What does privatisation mean?

2 What effects can privatisation have on:

a) the objectives of an industry?

b) the quality of goods and services?

c) competition and the price of products?

Business organisation

A Organisation in small and large businesses

1 key fact In a small business, communications can be direct and everyone can have a say in decisions.

- A small business (e.g. a local newsagent's) may have an owner and an assistant. Responsibility for decisions rests with the owner. The assistant may have a formal work contract, but most communications can be direct, verbal and informal.

- Communication in a small partnership can be informal, with all partners having an equal say in decisions.

2 key fact Larger businesses with more staff need a structure and more formal ways of communicating.

- Some set out to be **democratic** and **share responsibility** for decisions across the business. There may be internal structures based on groups with common interests, or on friendship groups.

- Most have a **hierarchical culture**, with decisions handed down to the many, from the few at the top.

3 key fact Hierarchical organisations have a clear chain of command from the most senior to junior staff.

- At each level, people take orders and instructions from above and give them to those below. Requests and complaints are sent upwards.

- Communications reflect the formal business culture, with many written notices and memos, formal reports and meetings with written agendas and minutes.

- It is thorough and detailed but may be expensive and time-consuming. Electronic communications have helped speed up and save money on formal communications.

owners
directors
managers
supervisors
operatives

B Organisation charts

① key fact Large businesses organise themselves in different ways.

The most common forms of organisation are:

- by **function** (based on people's roles, e.g. marketing, finance)
- by **product** (separate departments for each product, e.g. Ford vans, cars)
- by **geographical area** (local branches or national divisions, e.g. Ford UK, Ford Spain).

This is a typical organisation chart, showing a business divided up by function:

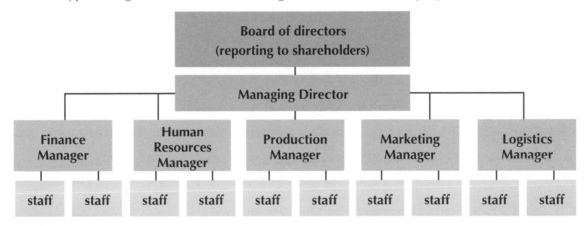

② key fact Span of control means the number of people over whom a person has direct authority.

A business with too long a chain of command, or with spans of control that are too wide, may find decision-making hard and rules difficult to enforce. **Delegation** is a common and efficient way of solving such problems. Authority for particular areas or tasks is passed down to a lower level. Control is clearest when everyone has a distinct role.

remember >>
Organisational structure must fit the needs of the business.

>> practice questions

The directors of Tolworth have reorganised their business: Jack Davis is now chairman; Paul Singh, finance manager; Daniel Davis, retail manager; Chris Davis, production manager and Irene Davis, managing director.

1 Draw an organisation chart showing the chain of command.

2 Your chart shows a division of labour within the company. Explain the term 'division of labour'.

3 List three business functions other than finance, retail and production.

4 Explain the terms 'chain of command' and 'span of control'.

5 State two job roles within the span of control of the finance manager.

6 State two advantages and two disadvantages of a hierarchical organisation.

Business production

- Business production covers the whole process from research to sales.
- Businesses may produce one product or sell a wide product mix.
- Large-scale production may cut costs for some businesses.

A Business production

① key fact   Business production describes the whole process.

The process begins with an idea for a new product. Research may suggest the best way of making or supplying the item. Investors provide capital for equipment, materials etc. Finally, the finished product is marketed, distributed and sold to customers.

② key fact   Business production involves the use of different resources.

- Materials: use of land, extraction of **raw materials**, materials from other businesses.
- Workers: a **labour** force is needed, in the UK or abroad.
- **Capital**: investment in machinery, buildings, vehicles.
- **Enterprise**: the owner(s) take the risk that the business will be a success.

B Product choice

>> key fact   Businesses may sell one product or have a wide product mix.

① **Sole product businesses** (e.g. a beef farmer):
- ✔ Good if the product is a quality one and hard to obtain.
- ✘ Can be risky if demand for the product suddenly falls.

② **Businesses with a wide product range** (e.g. a motor company):
- ✔ Customers have greater choice; the business spreads its risks.
- ✘ Can be difficult to manage on a large scale while keeping down costs.

③ **Businesses with a wide product mix** (e.g. Unilever):
- ✔ Risks are spread across many products in different markets.
- ✘ Can be difficult to manage products outside the business's core activity.

 **>> key fact** **Businesses need to assess their products' performance.**

The Boston Matrix provides a framework to assess sales growth and market share.

		Market share	
		High	Low
Market growth	Fast	**Stars** Likely to give good cash returns; need a lot of advertising	**Question marks** Difficult to be sure of their future; need lots of investment
	Slow	**Cash cows** Steady market; well-set products which can be 'milked' for profits	**Dogs** Poor market share; need to be killed off

C Scale of production

① key fact **Small firms can have higher costs but better service.**

- Producing goods on a small scale, fixed costs per product unit are high.
- Can offer personal and local service and specialist products.
- Can offer flexibility in meeting different demands.

 **② key fact** **Larger firms can take advantage of economies of sale.**

Economies of scale (reductions in unit costs when producing larger quantities) may be:

- **Technical** – large firms can use machinery more effectively.
- **Trading** – large firms can buy in bulk at favourable prices.
- **Financial** – large firms can usually borrow more at lower interest rates.
- **Managerial** – large firms can hire specialist highly skilled management.

③ key fact **Firms may become too large to manage efficiently.**

For example, a firm with many factories nationwide may develop communications problems, leading to inefficiency and increased costs.

>> practice questions

1 Identify supermarket products which could be matched to each of the Boston Matrix categories.

2 Explain how supermarkets benefit from economies of scale.

exam tip >>

Several ideas with examples are better than one long point.

Methods of production

- Businesses may choose a mix of job, batch and flow production methods.

- Just-in-time (JIT) production can be efficient if carefully managed.

A Choosing a production method

>> **key fact** Most businesses use a mix of production methods.

remember >>

Businesses often combine different production methods when making a range of products.

1. **Job production**: making a unique item from start to finish, e.g. house extension, ship.

   - Often a response to an individual order.

2. **Batch production**: larger-scale production of 'batches' of similar items, e.g. bread, clothing.

   - An entire batch of products is processed through a production stage before moving to the next stage.

   - Machinery is reset and a new batch of different items is then processed.

   - Production is aimed at the market rather than the individual customer.

3. **Flow (or mass) production**: continuous production of identical items, e.g. newspapers, cars.

   - The items flow through a set of specialised operations on an assembly line.

   - Division of labour is essential, with workers trained to do specialist tasks.

   - Production is aimed at the largest markets of all.

	Advantages	Disadvantages
Job production	High quality product made by skilled workers Job satisfaction high Easy to isolate problem areas	Expensive materials Expensive labour Slow process, machinery often idle Repeat orders unlikely
Batch production	Lower unit costs (increased scale of production) Flexibility possible in batch quantity, according to demand More specialised machinery with less idle time	Costly storage needed Some repetition in jobs Batches need to be moved Machinery needs resetting
Flow production	Large output, low unit cost Good use of production time Low-skilled, easily-trained labour Products of standard quality	Large investment in machinery Inflexible assembly line Repetitive work, poor motivation Products all the same Breakdowns cause big problems

B Just-in-time (JIT) production

>> **key fact** Just-in-time production is an efficient method if carefully managed.

✔
- JIT production is a relatively new development.
- Raw materials, parts and components are made available in just the right quantity.
- Each load arrives at the assembly line, fully quality-checked, just in time to be used.
- Computer-controlled information links are a vital part of the process.
- Can save time and money usually spent on storage/internal stock movement.

✖
- JIT needs very careful management and close ties with suppliers.
- Breakdowns in the system can cause costly delays.

remember >>

JIT methods won't suit every business.

C Teamwork

>> **key fact** In most production processes, teamwork is essential.

1. In batch or flow production, teams typically take charge of sections of the process.
2. The team controls the speed and quality of production.
3. The team can help to spot and sort out problems.
4. Greater job satisfaction can be gained if proper training is received.
5. Some computer-controlled processes have led to less teamwork, more part-time work, less job security and less satisfaction.

>> practice questions

Crown Fashions Ltd makes clothes for major high street stores. The stores require a range of sizes, colours and designs for each garment. To meet these requirements, Crown uses batch production methods.

1 What is batch production?

2 Why are batch production methods well suited to the manufacture of clothing?

exam tip >>

Remember to match each advantage you mention with an example from clothing manufacture.

Efficiency and new technology

 A business must be efficient to compete successfully.

 Efficiency can be increased by innovation and the use of new technology in the production process.

A Business efficiency

① key fact In a competitive world, a business must produce maximum output at minimum cost. This is known as efficient production.

- Efficiency is a measure of how well the production process is running.

- With some products, it is easy to measure the number produced by a worker or machine in a certain time.

- It is more difficult to measure efficiency when a business produces a service. Quality may be more important than quantity.

- Improvements in efficiency of production can come from automation (greater use of machinery), changing work practices and productivity deals with workers.

- A firm may need to invest in management training or reorganisation to become more efficient.

② key fact Different measures of efficiency are used by businesses.

1 **Productivity** e.g. output per team, per person, per man-hour, per machine.

2 **Unit costs** are total costs divided by quantity produced.

   - Falling unit costs: good sign of improving efficiency.

   - Rising unit costs: production costs up or fewer products made.

3 **Idle resources** e.g. machines and workers standing idle.

   Can be improved:

   - by changing work practices

   - by mechanisation

   - by use of part-time workers.

4 **Stock levels**

   - Too few stocks can lead to stoppages in production.

   - Too many stocks can lead to surplus goods that no one wants.

5 **Product quality** as measured by complaints or number of products returned to a business.

6 **Poor management** e.g. evidence of inefficiencies right across the factory.

> **remember >>**
>
> A comment such as 'this business is inefficient' is a judgement and needs a reason to support it.

B Computer technology in business production

① key fact **Computer-controlled technology has made big improvements in some industries.**

There are several different uses of computers in business production.

1 **CAM** (computer-aided manufacturing):

- In processes such as engineering, computers program machines.
- They complete work more accurately and for longer than humans.
- Robots are ideal for dangerous, dirty or heavy jobs.

2 **CAD** (computer-aided design):

- Products can now be designed on screen using complex 3-D models.
- Production processes can be planned in advance.
- Saves expensive research time; avoids costly mistakes.

3 **CIM** (computer-integrated manufacturing):

- CIM factories combine all the latest technological developments.
- Everything is controlled by computers.
- The computer-programming team replaces the old factory managers.
- Products can be made on a large scale but 'custom made' in assembly to meet individual customer needs.

② key fact **Computer technology has costs and benefits.**

- High investment costs can be covered by cutting labour costs.
- Benefits depend on selling large quantities of the product and how long the technology stays up to date.

>> practice questions

Beau Nurseries employs four production staff, three sales staff and ten part-timers, some on a seasonal basis. The company plans to expand and introduce automation, CAM and computer control systems into the hothouses in order to become more capital-intensive.

1 State the meaning of:
  a) automation   b) CAM   c) computer control systems.

2 How could these new technologies be used in the hothouses?

3 Explain the meaning of the term 'capital-intensive'.

4 How might the new technology affect the work of Beau employees?

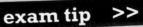

Quality management

- **Product quality is determined by businesses, their customers and the law.**

- **There are traditional and modern ways of managing quality production.**

A Deciding on the quality of a product

① key fact The quality of a product depends on its purpose.

All goods have to meet a purpose. Some, e.g. parachutes, need to be totally reliable. For others, e.g. clothes, appearance may be more important than quality.

② key fact Product quality is determined by businesses, customers and the law.

1 Businesses have different approaches to quality. They may try to make the best possible product or may want to compete on price.

2 Customers may expect a product to: last a long time; be fashionable in design; offer good back-up services from the producer; offer reasonable value for money.

3 The quality of a product can be set by law. Some products, e.g. car safety belts, must pass research checks before they can be sold. National standards are checked and enforced by government. All products must be fit for purpose as advertised at the point of sale.

B Sectors of business activity

① key fact Traditional quality control methods rely on sample checks by a specialist department.

Traditionally, the quality control department has been seen as responsible for improving and maintaining product quality. This includes monitoring machine performance, checking the quality of bought-in supplies and analysing the use of manpower.

② key fact Research and development (R & D) departments help develop new, high quality products.

R & D involves scientific research for new ideas/products. Many projects never reach a development stage. It takes time and money but may save costs in the long term. Usually only large, specialised companies can afford their own R & D departments.

C Modern quality control

>> **key fact** Businesses are increasingly using a system of total quality management (TQM) which makes all employees responsible for quality.

- New quality systems involve all staff in an overall 'quality policy'.

- The policy aims at 'zero defects' and tries to meet customers' needs.

- A modern quality management process cannot just be 'stuck on' to an old system.

- Good teamwork is required: a business with an open decision-making process finds the move to TQM much easier than those without.

- A top-quality process should: lead to good quality products; allow workers to operate safely; protect the environment; cut down waste.

remember >>

Quality management needs planning, training and, often, a change in production methods.

Traditional methods	**Post-production quality control**: controller randomly checks finished goods. Wasteful, as faults are only found at the end.
	Process control: controller samples products throughout the production process. Slight improvement.
Modern methods	**TQM**: everyone involved in the process. Improves staff motivation. Faults spotted/sorted out quickly. Costs are involved, though, as workers must be educated/trained to measure and monitor quality and seek improvement.
	Kaizen: a Japanese idea of continual improvement. Workers suggest improvements as often as possible so potential concerns are dealt with before they become problems. Voluntary groups ('quality circles') meet often to discuss ways of improving work and production.

>> practice questions

GRC employs seventy workers at its main factory making plastic moulded products for kitchens. All their products are made from plastic granules, which are melted and put into moulds. This process is computer controlled. On the other side of town, GRC has a smaller factory with a supervisor and six people employed in assembly and packaging.

1 GRC is considering moving assembly and packaging on to the main site. Do you think this is a good idea? Give reasons.

2 The production manager believes everyone should be involved in quality control.

a) What is meant by quality control?

b) Describe ways in which GRC might try to obtain a high standard of quality control.

Business finance

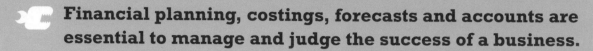

Financial planning, costings, forecasts and accounts are essential to manage and judge the success of a business.

Sources of finance can come from inside the business (internal) or outside (external).

A Importance of finance and financial management

1 key fact Finance is essential to any business.

Business owners need money to pay for:

- the **start-up costs** of buildings, equipment and materials
- the regular **running costs** such as electricity bills, employees' wages and taxes
- **unexpected events** such as breakdowns in equipment or accidents
- **investment** in new equipment or building expansion.

2 key fact Good financial management is essential to a business's survival.

- A good **business plan** must be written to back up a request for a loan.

- Estimates will need to be made to show when a business will **break even** and for what is considered a **reasonable price** for their product/service:
  - A product will **break even** at the point when the cost and revenue match.
  - A **reasonable price** is one when the consumer is prepared to pay the amount and the business is able to at least cover costs from this sale.

- Regular **cash flow forecasts and budgets** help to keep the business afloat on a month-by-month and year-by-year basis.

- **Detailed accounts** help managers to judge the success of the business activities.

> **remember >>**
> Business finance involves the interpretation of figures.

Case study

Mark and Megan have a sandwich business called Double M's. They rent a unit on a business park and sell directly to shops and local firms, offering working lunches.

When they first formed the business, they thought about all their start-up costs and their ongoing running costs. They decided how much money they needed to set up, and took a plan to the bank in case they needed a loan.

Mark and Megan make regular detailed costings, working out their costs and measuring them against revenue. These calculations show their break-even point and help them to set a price for their products, to give them a reasonable profit. They produce monthly cash flow forecasts which show them if they have the cash to pay monthly bills. They draw up business accounts to show how the figures work.

With all the details in front of them, Mark and Megan can measure the performance of their business and determine whether it is making a reasonable profit, or whether adjustments need to be made.

Sources of finance

Finance for a business can come from a variety of sources.

Some sources of finance are better for start-up costs; some are better for other costs, such as running costs. Financial sources can be grouped in different ways:

- by time period (short term or long term)
- whether the finance comes from inside the business (internal) or outside (external).

The table below compares internal and external sources of finance and their main use.

Source	Features	Used for
Internal		
Retained profit	Money saved out of net profit. No interest to pay; easily available. Most common source of finance.	Running costs. Also, potentially, renewal, expansion.
Investment	Money put in by owners or, if a limited company, obtained by selling shares. Usually long-term commitment.	Start-up costs, buying equipment, renewal, expansion.
Selling/leasing assets	A one-off for raising money, generally when a business is struggling.	Buying equipment, emergency running costs.
External		
Bank overdrafts	Money allowed to be withdrawn, despite account having negative balance. Short-term agreements, high interest charged.	Covering gaps in cash flow.
Loans	Money from banks etc. Arranged over different time periods; interest charged. Often need guarantees to ensure payback.	Start-up costs, buying equipment.
Grants	Money from government, generally tied in to fixed commitments such as improving a region's unemployment or environment.	Start-up costs, buying equipment, expansion
Trade credit	Buying goods, but not paying for them until an agreed later date.	Buying stock.
Hire purchase (HP)	HP or leasing payments spread over time, so less money committed in the short term. With HP, interest charged, but item eventually owned outright. With leasing, item never owned but can be updated/repaired easily.	Buying equipment, renewal.

>> practice questions

1 **Give three examples of internal and three of external sources of finance.**
2 **Why might restaurant owners seek a bank loan to pay for a second restaurant?**

Break even

- General running costs can be divided into fixed and variable costs.

- A break-even point can be found where revenue just covers costs.

- Break-even analysis helps a business to make decisions about prices, costs and the level of sales.

A Fixed and variable costs

1 key fact Businesses can divide general running costs into fixed and variable costs.

- **Fixed costs (overheads)** do not, in the short term, change with the number of goods or services produced, e.g. rent on buildings, rates to local councils, interest on loans.

  (NB if the business shrinks or expands drastically, then fixed costs will change.)

- **Variable costs** change with the amount of goods or services produced, e.g. cost of raw materials, parts, packaging.

2 key fact Some costs may be classified differently by different businesses.

Some costs (e.g. electricity, transport, wages) may be fixed costs for one business but variable costs for another. For example, power for a high street bank is a fixed cost, but for a launderette is a variable cost dependent on use of the washing machines. Over a longer period all costs could vary.

B Calculating the break-even point

1 key fact Fixed and variable costs are measured against sales revenue to calculate whether a business will make a profit or loss or if it will break even at different levels of sales.

2 key fact There are two commonly used ways to work out the break-even point.

1 The **contribution method** involves a two-part calculation:

   a) price per unit minus variable cost per unit (variable cost) = contribution (to cover fixed costs)

   b) Break-even point (level of sales) = fixed costs divided by contribution.

2 The **graph method** involves drawing lines to show costs at different outputs and expected revenue from different levels of sales. Break even is at the point where the lines cross.

> **remember >>**
>
> **Show your working out: you can get marks for method even if the calculation is wrong.**

a) Plot fixed costs (horizontal line at level of fixed costs). Then plot variable costs (diagonal line showing costs at different outputs).

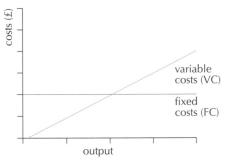

b) Plot total costs line (diagonal line showing total cost incurred per item; total costs = fixed costs + variable costs at any level of output).

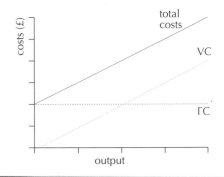

c) Add total revenue line (diagonal line showing revenue obtained per item sold) (the vertical axis represents revenue and the horizontal axis levels of sales).

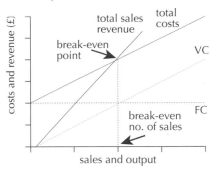

Key terms

- Variable costs = variable cost per unit × output level

- Total costs = fixed costs + variable costs

- Total revenue = price per unit × sales level

- Break-even point is when total costs = total revenue

C Making sense of break-even results

>> **key fact** Break-even results are used when considering pricing, cost-cutting, etc.

1 Current output below break even: can raise prices; cut costs; boost production.

2 Current output beyond break even: good margin of safety; could even lower prices.

3 Not breaking even: may not be a problem if the business/product is new. It takes time to cover start-up costs/get products known to customers.

>> practice questions

Double M's, the sandwich business, has fixed costs of £1000. The cost to produce a sandwich is £1 and the price charged for each sandwich is £2.

1 Give one example of a fixed cost for Double M's and one variable cost.

2 Explain the term 'break even'. How many sandwiches must be sold to break even?

3 What happens to the break-even point if:

a) The price of a sandwich is reduced to £1.50?

b) A cheaper bread supplier is found, reducing production costs to 60p?

c) Fixed costs increase to £1200 per month?

Cash flow

- A business needs enough cash to cover its immediate needs.

- A cash flow forecast predicts money coming in and going out over a fixed period.

A Why cash is important

1 **key fact** A business needs enough money to cover its immediate needs.

- **Cash** in the bank is a **liquid asset** that allows a firm to buy the goods and services it needs, add value to them, trade and make profits.

- A firm might be making profits, but if it does not have enough cash to pay its **creditors** (people it owes), it can be declared **insolvent** by the courts and may have to cease trading.

- Every year thousands of businesses fail as a result of cash flow problems.

2 **key fact** Cash flows can be compared to water flowing into and out of a bath.

The cash coming in is like water from a tap. Cash going out is like water out of the plughole. The task is to keep a reasonable level of water in the bath.

Cash in
Start-up capital; cash from sales of goods/services; bank loans; grants, etc.

Cash out
Raw materials or stock; fixed costs; tax payments; equipment; wages/salaries, etc.

B Cash flow forecasts

1 **key fact** A cash flow forecast is a way of predicting cash in and cash out over a fixed period.

Generally presented as a chart or graph, a cash flow enables established businesses to check whether or not a cash crisis is looming. It is also vital to the business plan presented by a new company to a potential lender. On a chart, cash inflows (receipts) are listed first, followed by cash outflows (payments).

remember >>
Profit is a surplus from trading activities. Cash is an asset that can be used to pay debts.

key fact Interpretation of a cash flow chart is important for a business.

- Negative closing balance (a deficit): indicates not enough cash to pay the bills.

- Regular large surplus: suggests the business could repay some debts or buy new stocks or equipment.

- Credit sales: payment for goods/services is not received until some time after the sale.

- Buying goods on credit: goods arrive before payment is due.

Here is a cash flow forecast chart of a company with an opening January balance of £0:

	January	February	March	April
Cash in	9500	7000	4000	4000
minus **Cash out**	7400	6500	6600	5500
equals **Net cash flow**	2100	500	−2600	−1500
plus **Opening balance**	0	2100	2600	0
equals **Closing balance**	2100	2600	0	−1500

>> practice questions

A soft toy company, Fuzz, has drawn up an actual cash flow graph for the last six months' trading, to compare with its forecast for the same period.

1 What does the cash flow forecast graph show?

2 How did the actual cash flow differ from the forecast?

3 What problems might these differences cause for Fuzz?

4 How might Fuzz improve its cash flow?

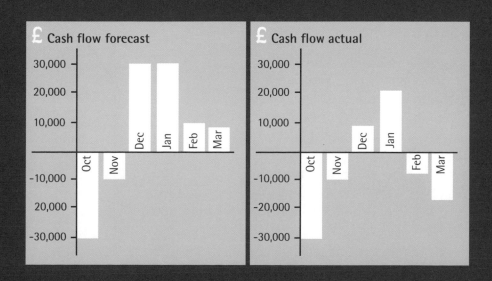

Financial statements

A The importance of financial accounts

>> **key fact** All businesses need an efficient system for keeping track of their money.

The profit and loss account and the balance sheet are the two main financial statements.

- Both provide information on recent business activity.

- Both show how these activities have been paid for.

- This information can be compared with figures from previous years to assist decision-making about the future.

- Small firms draw up their own financial statements or pay an accountant to do it.

- Larger companies have their own finance department.

- By law, all companies must provide shareholders with accounting information.

- Public limited companies do this through the annual report and accounts.

B Profit and loss account

A record of revenue (money in) and costs (money out) during the past accounting period.

Trading account
Shows gross profit (sales revenue minus cost of sales).

Profit and loss account
Shows net profit (gross profit plus other income, e.g. interest or sales of assets, minus overheads).

Appropriation account
Shows what happened to net profit (e.g. paid out as tax, dividends to shareholders, retained profit).

Profit and loss account
for year ended 31 Mar 2009

		£000
	Sales revenue	18 200
(-)	Cost of sales	10 100
	Gross profit	8100
(+)	Other income	500
(-)	Overheads	4500
	Net profit	4100
(-)	Tax	1000
	Profits after tax	3100
	Dividends paid	1800
	Retained profit	1300

Government uses this figure to decide how much tax should be paid.

Lenders, shareholders, etc. can see how well a business is doing from this figure, and can weigh up the risks of further investment.

A record of the value of what a firm owns (its assets), what it owes (its liabilities) and the value of the capital invested in the firm. It is a 'snapshot' taken at a particular point in time (usually the last day of the accounting period).

Assets (e.g. buildings and equipment). May be different views of how much such things are worth.

Assets which are easily turned into cash.

Debts to be repaid within one year (e.g. short-term loans).

Current assets minus current liabilities.

Total assets minus current liabilities.

Long-term loans, etc. Balance sheet layout varies between firms – these liabilities, instead of being subtracted here, are often added to the capital and reserves section below.

Owners' or share capital, retained profit, loans, grants etc.

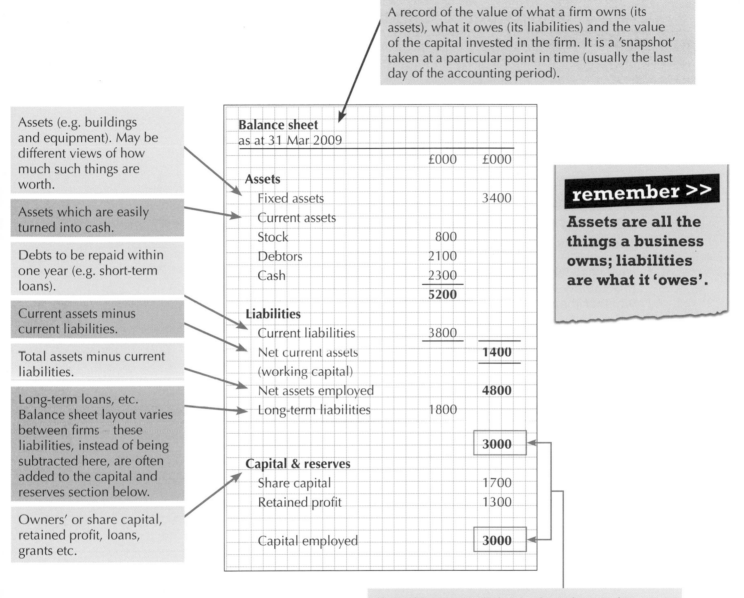

Balance sheet as at 31 Mar 2009	£000	£000
Assets		
Fixed assets		3400
Current assets		
Stock	800	
Debtors	2100	
Cash	2300	
	5200	
Liabilities		
Current liabilities	3800	
Net current assets (working capital)		**1400**
Net assets employed		**4800**
Long-term liabilities	1800	
		3000
Capital & reserves		
Share capital		1700
Retained profit		1300
Capital employed		**3000**

These figures must balance: the 'where is the money now' and 'where did the money come from' boxes must tally.

>> practice questions

You are an accountant. A friend asks you about financial statements. Can you answer their questions (below)?

1 What will tell us whether or not we can pay off our debts?

2 What will tell us whether or not we can expand?

Financial performance

⚡ Managers can check on financial performance by taking the accounts information for the past year and doing some comparisons and investigations with the figures.

⚡ Detailed information on financial performance is provided by performance ratios.

A The importance of performance ratios

>> **key fact** Businesses should always be aware of the condition of their finances, so they can make any necessary adjustments to keep afloat.

- Managers need to have more precise knowledge about a company's profitability and liquidity than just whether it is making money and whether it has enough cash to pay off its debts.

- Managers might need to know if it is making enough money given the level of sales or money invested.

- They might need to know what percentage of available cash would be needed to pay off its debts.

- This detailed information is provided by performance ratios.

- Ratios are worked out by comparing different pairs of figures in the accounts that are related in some way.

- Each ratio gives slightly different information about the profitability or liquidity of a business.

Which of these two companies has the better performance?

	Sales	Profits
Company A	£10 million	£1 million
Company B	£200 million	£8 million

remember >>
Ratios are based on past figures. They can help with forecasts but will not guarantee results.

remember >>
Some ratios are shown in figures, e.g. 1:3, others are written as %.

B Different kinds of performance ratios

Ratio	What does it show?	Who might be interested?
Profitability		
Gross profit margin Gross profit : sales revenue $\dfrac{\text{Gross profit}}{\text{Sales revenue}} \times 100\%$	Gross profit for every £1 of sales. The bigger the %, the greater the profit.	Managers – is the firm performing well? Creditors – are profits enough to repay loans?
Net profit margin Net profit : sales revenue $\dfrac{\text{Net profit}}{\text{Sales revenue}} \times 100\%$	As before, but now allowing for fixed costs.	As before.
Return on capital employed (ROCE) Net profit : capital employed $\dfrac{\text{Net profit}}{\text{Capital employed}} \times 100\%$	Profit created from each £1 invested.	Shareholders (investors) – is investment providing as good a return as other options might?
Liquidity		
Current ratio Current assets : current liabilities	How easily a firm's short-term debts could be paid from current assets. Ratio of 1:1 means a firm is just covering its debts. Ratio of 3:1 means it has three times the money needed to cover its debts. This is wasteful: the money could buy machinery, etc.	Managers, creditors – how easily can the firm's debts be covered? Linked to cash flow forecasts (see page 34).
Acid test ratio Current assets – stock : current liabilities	Current assets figures include stocks, which might be hard to turn into ready cash. Acid test, which removes them from the equation, is a more realistic measure. A reasonable figure is seen as between 0.5:1 and 1:1.	As before.

>> practice questions

Examine this extract from a balance sheet.

1 Calculate the company's current ratio.

> **exam tip >>**
>
> This should be written in the form A : B.

2 What does this ratio tell you about the success of the company?

Balance sheet as at 31.3.09		
	£000	£000
Fixed assets		13 000
Current assets		
Stock	3880	
Debtors	40	
Cash	80	
	4000	
Current liabilities		
Creditors	720	
Overdraft	80	
	800	

People in business

Managing people is vitally important: in a small business, managers have direct responsibility; in larger businesses, the Human Resource department assumes a part of this role.

A Managing people

1 **key fact** People are vital assets in a business and need to be managed effectively.

- The largest expenditure in most businesses is staff wages. Recruitment, training and the creation of good working relationships need careful management.

- In a small business, these responsibilities are usually held by the manager.

- In a large business, a Human Resource (HR) department is largely responsible for people management.

2 **key fact** HR departments carry out a wide range of tasks.

- These include: recruiting and training staff; preparing employment contracts, including legal requirements; dealing with negotiations between staff over pay and working conditions; supervising health and safety concerns.

Case study

A typical day for a Human Resource Manager at the head office of a computer retailer.

1 Analyses results of a new bonus pay scheme. Sorts through job applications with the finance manager and arranges interviews.

2 Gives new sales staff employment contracts, shows them around and introduces them to their new colleagues.

3 Arranges a meeting with the despatch department to discuss a complaint over new teams.

4 Has a meeting with management and Union representatives to discuss teleworking from home for employees who work on the telephone all day.

During the day, deals with numerous phone calls, carries out a health and safety check on the office areas and spends time arranging the staff Christmas party.

B What motivates people to work?

 key fact Successful businesses have managers who understand how to motivate their staff.

People have different reasons for working. These include:

- earning money to survive and to pay for interesting activities
- providing social contact with other people
- as a vocation, giving purpose to life.

 key fact Motivation theories offer explanations for human behaviour.

Maslow's Hierarchy of Needs

- Abraham Maslow analysed why people work. He drew a 'Hierarchy of Needs' pyramid from his findings.

- He ranked people's needs in order of importance, with the most basic at the bottom of the pyramid, and more advanced ones at the top.

- Maslow's theory suggests people won't be happy at work unless basic needs are met. For workers to stay motivated, they need to feel self-fulfilled, perhaps by being given responsibilities.

Other theories suggest the attitudes of employers and employees may be the most important influences on motivation.

Self-fulfilment needs (reaching your potential)

Self-esteem needs (a sense of status)

Social needs (relationships with other workers)

Safety needs (job security, pension)

Basic needs / **S**urvival (food and shelter or money to obtain these)

>> practice questions

'The pay is poor, the hours long and I have to work at weekends.'

'Everybody tells me what to do ... it is no fun.'

1 What do these statements suggest about the motivation of hotel workers?

2 Identify and explain two possible ways in which workers' motivation could be improved.

Motivation and pay

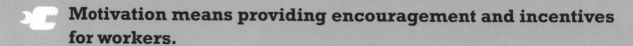

- Motivation means providing encouragement and incentives for workers.

- This can be achieved through different kinds of payment system.

A Financial and non-financial incentives

>> **key fact** Work incentives can be both financial and non-financial.

- Incentives affect people's commitment to work.

- Higher pay is an incentive to a person who works just for money, but it may also help motivate someone who is working for other reasons.

Financial incentives	Non-financial incentives
• receiving a good wage • bonus payments, e.g. for meeting targets • fringe benefits, e.g. free meals • extra payments, e.g. overtime • commission, e.g. for the number of goods sold • a long-term contract • payments in the form of company shares	• varied and interesting work • responsibility to make decisions • being praised for good work • promotion opportunities • feeling listened to and valued • good working environment • feeling challenged by the work

B Motivation and pay

>> **key fact** Different pay systems can influence the commitment of workers.

1. **Wages and salaries** – wages (most manual workers) are based on hourly rates, and are normally paid weekly. Salaries (most non-manual workers) are based on yearly figures, and paid directly into bank accounts each month. In both cases, income tax (PAYE in Britain) and National Insurance are deducted by the employer, and paid to the government. Some governments have set a national minimum (basic) wage.

2. **Time rate** – payment for the time taken to complete a job. Can encourage workers to take longer finishing a job to boost their pay.

3. **Overtime** – payment when a job cannot be completed in the normal time, often paid at a higher rate than normal.

4 **Piece rate** – payment for the number of products finished. Can encourage speed but may reduce quality.

5 **Bonus payments** – extra payments if a job is finished early or by a specified deadline.

6 **Commission** – payment of a (low) basic wage plus a percentage of the value of items sold or made. This is common practice in sales jobs.

7 **Performance-related pay** – another form of payment by results, where pay is linked to achievement of targets. Difficult to use in jobs where targets are not easily measured (e.g. nurses caring for different numbers of patients, with different levels of need).

8 **Profit-sharing** – extra payments based on company profit over a given period.

9 **Fringe benefits** – these include company cars, pensions, private healthcare, cheap loans. Managers are more likely to receive these than workers.

>> practice questions

1 **Which type of payment and/or fringe benefits would be most suitable for the following workers? Give your reasons.**

   a) a cleaner

   b) a salesperson

   c) a nurse

   d) a shop assistant

   e) a lorry driver

2 **A mobile phone business has just appointed a junior manager and wants her to stay for several years. What kind of incentives could the company use to encourage her to stay with them?**

Recruitment

> The process of finding new staff must be well run to avoid wasting company time.

> Choosing the right person for a job largely depends on getting the right procedures and documents in place.

A The recruitment process

① key fact A small business will recruit on a personal basis. Good working relationships between partners are vital. A new recruit is likely to work on many different tasks.

② key fact Larger businesses must plan ahead to identify and fill job vacancies.

Vacancies arise for a variety of reasons, some planned and some unplanned. These include: retirement; promotion; the creation of new jobs through business expansion.

③ key fact The recruitment process can be seen as a set of separate stages.

The typical stages for a medium to large company are outlined below. A small company may not follow all of the procedures.

Step 1

The manager with the vacancy and the HR manager write a job description and person specification.

Step 2

A job advertisement is placed in a suitable publication. After the application deadline, CVs are checked to remove unsuitable applicants. The rest are compared to the person specification to arrive at a shortlist for interview.

Step 3

Candidates are interviewed, and may be given an appropriate test. The job is offered to the most suitable person (or readvertised if no candidate proves suitable). Unsuccessful candidates are notified.

Step 4

The successful candidate's references are checked. If any problems arise, the job may be offered to the next most suitable person from the list. If references are fine, a date is set for the new person to start.

remember >>

Job adverts and interviews must be in line with the law on equal opportunities.

Step 5

A contract and induction training are arranged. The performance of the new staff member is monitored via an appraisal system – manager and worker agree on targets for a set period, then review the results.

B Recruitment documents

>> **key fact** Recruitment documents must be carefully written.

- Job descriptions are often used for years to identify the right skills, and to assess a person in their job.

- The wording must be accurate, fair and clear in its meaning.

- Candidates should take the same care writing applications or providing CVs.

The key contents of some recruitment documents are described below.

Job description:

drawn up by an employer

Lists all the duties the employee must carry out, as well as:
- the job title
- who they are responsible to
- who they are in charge of.

Person specification:

drawn up by an employer

Outlines the ideal candidate, and is used to find a person to fill the vacancy. Contains things like:
- qualifications required
- previous experience needed
- special skills needed, e.g. foreign languages
- personality needed, e.g. good telephone manner/confident nature for a receptionist.

Job advertisement:

written by an employer

Contains details of a position to be filled, and where to apply. May be:
- internal – only circulated within the business to give existing staff the chance to apply
- external – advertised in local, national or specialist newspapers, Job Centres, recruitment agencies.

CV (curriculum vitae):

written by a job applicant

Normally laid out like this:
- name
- date of birth
- address and telephone number
- educational qualifications
- previous jobs (starting with the most recent)
- interests
- names of referees (one is usually the last employer, or headteacher if the applicant is a school leaver).

>> practice questions

Explain the importance of a job description and an interview as part of the recruitment process.

exam tip >>

It is helpful to refer to a particular job as an example.

Recruitment case study

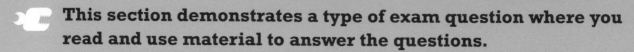

This section demonstrates a type of exam question where you read and use material to answer the questions.

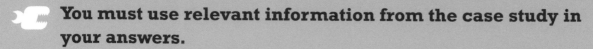

You must use relevant information from the case study in your answers.

Study all the information here, and use it to give full answers to the questions that follow.

- Kim works for a computer company called Bytes, which sells from retail outlets and by mail order, and gives full after-sales support. She needs someone to work at the main warehouse, running the shop at the front and also giving advice and technical support to customers over the phone.

- Kim and a colleague have drawn up the job description and person specification shown below. Having tried to recruit internally without success, she then placed an advertisement in the local paper. She has now narrowed down her shortlist to two candidates. Their CVs are shown opposite.

Job description

Title: Customer service representative

Responsible to: Sales manager

Responsible for: no staff

Function

- To sell hardware and software in the shop.

- To provide technical advice to customers.

Duties

- Start up demonstration machines in the shop each morning.

- Greet and assist customers.

- Demonstrate the use of the display machines and software.

- Operate the till and process cash and credit payments.

- Switch off all machines at the end of the day.

- Provide relief cover for telephone technical support staff when instructed.

Person specification

Position: Customer service representative

Educational qualifications

Essential:	5 GCSEs at grades A*–C to include either Business Studies or Computing
Desirable:	A level or vocational qualification in ICT
Experience:	Previous retail experience preferred
Special skills:	An interest in computers and good knowledge of current market for PCs and software
Personality:	Polite, pleasant personality

Curriculum Vitae

Paula Tait

Date of Birth: 10th June 1990

10, High Street, Evesham

Qualifications:

GCSE English B

French A

Maths D

Science C

Business Studies C

Employment:

2006 to date: Sales Assistant, Tesco, Evesham

Interests:

Riding, walking

References:

Head teacher, Courtmoor School, Evesham

Curriculum Vitae

Karen Lewis

Date of Birth: 29th May 1990

The Pines, Main Street, Evesham

Qualifications:

GCSE	English	C
	Maths	C
	ICT	A
	Business Studies	B
	Art	C
GNVQ	Intermediate Business	merit

Employment:

To date – three weeks' work experience at a computer shop, plus Saturday work this year at the same shop.

Interests:

Music, computing

References:

The Manager, Your PC, Evesham

>> practice questions

1 **If you were Kim, which of the two candidates would you interview and why?**

2 **List six questions you would ask at interview.**

3 **What does the term 'recruit internally' mean? What are the advantages of this?**

Training staff

- Training is an important business activity which benefits both employers and employees.

- It can involve both new and experienced staff and take place on or off the job.

A Why training is important

>> **key fact** Training costs money but helps produce good quality staff and a good reputation for a business.

It is important for a variety of reasons:

1 An employer may have to buy expert guidance and pay staff while they train.

2 Unemployed people may have to develop their skills to help them get jobs.

3 People need training to cope with a new job.

4 Ongoing staff training is essential, as the business environment is constantly changing.

5 Workers need to acquire new skills and work flexibly.

6 Properly trained staff:

- are more productive and satisfied in their work

- take less time off and stay longer with a business, becoming experienced and highly skilled

- have confidence in their ability and are more likely to obtain promotion.

7 A business with a good training reputation is respected by staff, other employers and customers.

> **remember >>**
> Training may cost money now but could benefit a business for years.

B Induction training

>> **key fact** Induction training helps new employees settle into a business.

Induction training is given to new employees. It teaches them the basic skills required for the job, introduces them to the business and its expectations, may include a company presentation, e.g. a video, and can involve experienced employees acting as mentors to new recruits.

Case study

The first day at work

Karen receives a staff handbook on her first day. She is shown around and meets her new colleagues. She watches a video about the company and is shown how to use the display computers and the till.

C Training can take place on and off the job

Training can take place on the job or away from work.

1 **On-the-job training**: given while employees are working.

- May involve an employee being guided through a process.

- May also involve mentoring when an employee is teamed up with an experienced colleague (to discuss problems and progress).

- Skilled training staff may organise activities, e.g. group problem-solving tasks, role-playing.

2 **Off-the-job training**: specialist training which involves employees stopping their usual work.

- Often provided by another company at a training centre.

- Saves a business from having to employ its own training staff.

- Is useful when new technology requires specialist skills beyond the reach of a business.

- May be expensive to buy.

- Employees may be unwilling to travel/put up with the inconvenience.

D Government training schemes

Government schemes can improve workers' qualifications and help get the unemployed back to work.

- Learning and Skills Councils manage training in regional areas. Grants are available for businesses promoting certain kinds of training, especially in IT.

- Investors in People (IIP) awards recognise quality training in businesses which set high standards, involve staff and evaluate their own success regularly.

- National Vocational Qualifications (NVQs) are awarded to people acquiring specific job skills, assessed in the workplace to set standards. Different levels of NVQ range from beginner to university-level.

- Modern apprenticeships are available for 16- to 25-year-olds to encourage vocational training at work.

- A 'new deal' government programme aimed at younger people and the long-term unemployed offers the option of more training, subsidised employment and voluntary work. Claimants lose benefits if they don't take part.

>> practice questions

1 **Why is on-the-job training most likely to be used when a new worker joins a small business?**

2 **Why might a company pay for off-the-job training to teach its employees to use new software?**

exam tip   >>

You can explain the benefits for both the company and the employees.

49

Communication at work

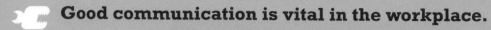

- Good communication is vital in the workplace.

- ICT has speeded up many forms of communication.

A Internal and external communication

① key fact Businesses need to communicate with staff internally and with customers and suppliers outside.

> **Internal communication**
> Good communication within an organisation enables people to do their jobs effectively (e.g. a good manager will explain clearly what a team member has to do).

> **External communication**
> Good communication between a business and its customers keeps customers loyal (e.g. a business needs to tell customers when their goods will arrive).

② key fact Many businesses have customer service staff who specialise in external communication with customers.

- Business order forms can be complicated and it is worth giving specialist help to customers. This avoids expensive deliveries of the wrong goods and keeps customers returning.

- Customers can lose time and money through poor business communications. Good customer service prevents costly court claims and compensation payments.

B Channels of communication

① key fact The success of messages depends largely on organisation and choice of message type.

- The way a message is passed is called the channel of communication.

Written channels	Verbal channels
memo; letter; e-mail; fax; notice; report	meeting; telephone call; conversation; presentation; public address system
Written communications provide a permanent record on paper or disk.	Verbal communications provide speedy feedback and are especially good for negotiations.

key fact A business needs to use the right kind of channel in the right direction.

Some channels fit their purpose and direction very well. For example:

- notices used as 'downwards' messages (from management to staff)

- reports used as 'upwards' messages (from staff to management)

- memos and emails used as 'sideways' messages (between colleagues).

C The importance of ICT

>> key fact ICT has changed the way people work.

1) A personal computer with word processing, spreadsheets and databases allows a worker to write, process complex data and keep detailed records quickly and efficiently.

2) With a broadband connection, information can be sent through the telephone network, giving email facilities and access to the Internet.

3) Internet access is also vital to those who work at home using computer technology to connect them to their employers. The employer can save on costs and employees can choose flexible working hours.

4) Suppliers and customers can contact businesses through websites worldwide.

remember >>

Today, both speed and accuracy are required in most communications.

>> practice questions

1 What are the main advantages and disadvantages of home working for:

a) the employer?   b) the employee?

2 What advantages does a business website offer to:

a) the business?   b) the customer?

Industrial relations

- Good industrial relations are vital to modern workplaces.

- Trade unions/trade associations can help to represent workers and employers.

- The law provides a framework for good working conditions.

A Good industrial relations

① key fact In successful businesses, employers and workers respect each others' rights and decision making is fair.

- Industrial relations describe the relationship between the workforce and the management of a business. Good relations mean difficult decisions are resolved openly and fairly.

- In any business, issues involving staff and management might be small (e.g. lateness), or more important and affect the whole workforce (e.g. pay negotiations).

- Businesses, especially large ones, need good organisation and a clear line of responsibility so that everyone knows what to do or who to talk to about problems.

② key fact Employers and workers have different interests as well as shared concerns.

Everyone wants their business to be a success, but employers may be more concerned about cutting costs and selling products for profit. Workers may worry more about decent working conditions and a good pay packet. Both groups have to balance the protection of their own interests with their shared concern to meet customers' expectations.

B Trade unions and trade associations

>> key fact Trade unions and trade associations represent workers and employers in discussions and disputes.

- Trade unions look after the interests of the workers. Many people join a union because it will negotiate on their behalf, dealing with issues such as pay, holiday entitlement, redundancy and job security. Unions offer bargaining skills; services such as legal help in cases of unfair dismissal; advice on work-related matters; benefits such as cheaper insurance or personal loans.

- Trade associations speak on behalf of employers. There are over one hundred large associations and many smaller ones. Employers as a whole are represented by the CBI (Confederation of British Industry). They can negotiate pay; present the industry's view to the public; provide advice for firms.

C Industrial relations, employment and the law

>> **key fact** The law provides a framework for good working conditions.

- There have been many changes in the workplace in recent years. Few employers can offer a guaranteed job for life and many firms prefer to take workers as and when they need them.

- To ensure the fair treatment of all workers and responsible behaviour of all in the workplace, the government has created employment laws.

remember >>

Many firms protect their workers with better policies than the law demands.

Things an employer must do	Things an employer must not do
Provide a written statement on pay, holidays and period of employment	Discriminate against workers on grounds of race, age, gender or disability (Equal Opportunities Laws)
Give equal pay to men and women if they are doing the same work	Stop a worker from belonging to a trade union
Give specific benefits to workers who have completed two years with the firm	Employ children under 13
Follow health and safety laws (Health and Safety at Work Act, 1974)	Dismiss a worker unfairly

Health and safety points to remember:

- Employers must provide fire escapes, safety guards on machines and good toilets. Good overall hygiene standards should be kept.

- Employers and employees should take reasonable care to look after their own and others' safety.

- Employers must identify harmful tasks and minimise risks.

Equal opportunities points to remember:

Employers must show no discrimination on grounds of race, age, gender or disability in their:

- selection procedures
- training
- selection for redundancy.
- contracts
- benefits

remember >>

You don't need to know names and dates of employment laws but must know what is expected of firms.

>> practice questions

Kimberly's paint factory pays well but workers have no protective clothing in the fume-filled mixing section and no workers have written contracts. In what ways is this employer breaking the law and how could a trade union help the workers?

Negotiating

- Most industries/businesses resolve issues (e.g. pay) by collective bargaining.

- Successful negotiations usually require compromise.

- Industrial action is difficult and costly but felt to be necessary at times.

A Collective bargaining

>> **key fact** Most industries and businesses decide pay and other issues by collective bargaining.

- Bargaining may be done at a national level, as with a nationwide industry, or at a local level with an individual business.

- Local negotiation may involve a small firm's union representative (sometimes called the shop steward) bargaining with management on behalf of company workers.

- Generally, different unions within a company will have their own representatives, who negotiate for their own workers.

- Some Far Eastern companies with factories in the UK have introduced new-style agreements with just one union to represent all workers.

- Some firms ask workers to sign no-strike agreements and put more emphasis on teamwork.

B Negotiation and compromise

>> **key fact** Successful negotiations between groups usually require some compromise.

Employers and workers need good working relationships. Where they disagree over issues like pay or conditions, the different groups put their case firmly but usually agree to give way on some issues in return for agreement on others.

Case study

Talks on pay and machines are being held between a group of workers and their employer from a company making pre-packed cakes to sell to supermarkets. To stay in business, the cakes need to be made faster and at less cost.

Employer wants:
- new machinery to save costs
- wages 2% up if workers also train to use machines
- wages 2% up if more cakes are made

Skilled workers want:
- a 10% pay rise to stay ahead of the others
- new machines if they are the ones to use them

Unskilled workers:
- want 7% pay rise
- don't want to work with new machines

?

C Industrial action

If negotiations fail, more direct action can be taken.

1 Employers may close a factory. A union can call for industrial action to be taken. In either case, there are costs:

- Employers lose: production is stopped and customers may be lost.

- Workers lose: they won't be paid while on strike and may risk losing their jobs.

2 A union can call for its members to take industrial action, to try to pressurise management to accept the union's point of view. Unions must seek their members' opinions through a secret ballot (vote) before taking industrial action. Such action might involve a:

- strike (all workers stop work)

- ban on overtime

- boycott (of particular tasks)

- work to rule (only doing the tasks specified in your contract).

3 If agreement still can't be reached, the business might ask for help from ACAS (the Arbitration and Conciliation Advisory Service). They can provide independent people to conciliate (try to get the two sides to meet and discuss things) and arbitrate (decide what should be done.

remember >>

There is no guarantee that arbitration will produce the result wanted by employers or by a union.

>> practice questions

1 How might a large firm making chocolate bars be affected by:

a) an overtime ban?

b) a work to rule by some workers?

c) an all-out strike?

2 Why might a 'single union agreement' be good for both employers and workers in a large firm?

exam tip >>

Explain any assumptions behind your answer.

Business and marketing

- In a competitive business world, a product needs to be marketed.
- A business needs to research information about its future prospects.

A The importance of business competition

>> **key fact** Businesses generally compete with rivals to sell products.

① Competition creates choice for consumers.

② Competition encourages businesses to keep down costs.

B The importance of marketing

>> **key fact** In a competitive business world, a product needs to be marketed so consumers find out about it and buy it.

① Small businesses often use word of mouth and local advertising; big businesses often spend large amounts on marketing and use national advertising.

② Marketing activities involve:

- finding out about consumer tastes and opinions

- providing the right products in the right place at the right time

- promoting the products to inform and persuade consumers to buy.

③ Marketing has limits: no amount of packaging will sell a poor product longer term.

remember >>

A well-designed product may not sell well if marketing is poor.

Key features of marketing	Example: marketing a children's DVD
Most businesses are market-orientated: they make what consumers want at a price that sells.	The new products must look good, be affordable, and have characters/themes which appeal to the age group.
Consumers can be grouped into market segments. Advertising and prices can be targeted at the group most likely to buy the product.	The DVD will be wanted by children, but bought by parents. Advertise in comics and kids TV. Use high street poster campaigns.
Clever promotion (attractive packaging, links with celebrities and spin-off products) can all extend a product's life cycle and sales.	A toy character free with a DVD or special Christmas packaging can keep the product in the public eye.
Price is a key factor: a business must set a price to cover costs, make a profit and compete with rivals.	Although just 1p different, £7.99 may sound cheaper than £8.00. Two DVDs for the price of one may help to sell older products.

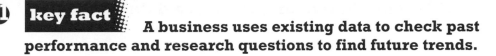

C Researching past and future performance

1 **key fact** A business uses existing data to check past performance and research questions to find future trends.

Information on past performance:
- are sales up or down on last year?
- has our market share increased?
- have our profits increased?
- why did this product fail?
- which products did best?

Information on current status:
- how much market share do we have?
- who is buying our products?
- why are they buying them?
- are our prices competitive?
- is advertising reaching the right people?
- are customers satisfied with quality?
- is someone else's product selling better?
- which of our products are selling best?

Information on future trends:
- can we keep sales going on existing products?
- can we launch a new product?
- which groups should we aim it at?
- what share of the market can we expect to win?
- are competitors planning new products?
- are there any new competitors?
- are there any new laws or technologies to consider?

2 **key fact** SWOT analysis helps a business examine its strengths and weaknesses.

SWOT analysis can be used to look at market position and how this could be improved. It reminds a business of its advantages over rivals, but these may not last.

Strengths and Weaknesses	Internal factors over which a business has some control, e.g. costs of overheads, materials and labour	A rival company produces a good range of family cars. Unit costs are high in the UK.
Opportunities and Threats	External factors over which a business has little or no control, e.g. the performance of a competitor, new government legislation	Our business is struggling and a takeover is threatened by a Chinese rival. The government is looking to see if UK companies are setting car prices too high.

>> practice questions

Mobile phones produced by a large European company are not selling as well as they were. What information should the company research to help it decide on its future?

exam tip >>

Use the SWOT framework to organise your answer.

Market research

Businesses classify their customers for research purposes.

Research involves analysing primary or secondary data.

Surveys can provide quantitative or qualitative data.

A Market segments

>> **key fact** **Businesses divide customers into groups (market segments), according to different characteristics.**

A business may want to know which sex or age group is particularly keen on a product. This gives them a target audience for their advertising, and helps in refining the product.

❶ **Socio-economic market segments**, used by government and many businesses, are based on characteristics of income, education and occupation:

Groups A, B	Professionals, managerial	15% of population
Groups C, D	Supervisory, clerical, skilled manual	75%
Groups E, Other	Unskilled manual, unemployed	10%

❷ **Focus groups** bring together typical customers of a particular product to find their opinions about the product. They can be based on gender, age, race or lifestyle and are used increasingly by businesses.

B Desk and field research

>> **key fact** **Research involves collecting and analysing information. It can be expensive and time-consuming.**

- **Field research**: collecting and analysing information gained first-hand, via interviews or surveys (primary data).

- **Desk research**: working with existing material, e.g. rivals' published accounts (secondary data).

| Primary data (original) | Up-to-date, directly relevant to products. Targeted at customers of a business. Remains confidential to a business. Can be expensive. |
| Secondary data (published) | Wide range of general data available. Quick to handle. Usually free. Can be out-of-date or off-target. |

remember >>
The speed at which a business can obtain information is important.

58

C Different kinds of surveys, questions and results

>> **key fact** When deciding which type of survey to use, quantity of response must be weighed against quality.

1 Types of survey

- One-on-one surveys: usually street or telephone questionnaires (good for quantity of data) or longer in-depth interviews (good for quality).
- Postal surveys: easy to set up, but usually low response rates and low quality of data.
- Group surveys: people meet to discuss a product (high quality, low quantity data).
- Random survey: each person (in a given area) has an equal chance of selection.
- Survey based on quotas: a set number of people from each market segment are interviewed.
- Targeted surveys: questions are put to one particular market segment.

2 Types of question

- Closed: the interviewee chooses from a set of possible answers, e.g. multiple-choice questions or scales. Answers are easy to analyse, but provide limited data.
- Open: no preset answers. Answers can be more valuable but are harder to analyse.

3 Results

- Quantitative information is easily presented as graphs or charts, e.g. to show which groups are buying a product most.
- Qualitative information gives detail and depth, and data is often presented as examples or case studies, e.g. to explain why a product appeals to a particular group.

>> practice questions

A petrol station is planning to expand its payment area to include a small shop, offering a range of services and products.

1 The petrol station manager wants to know the age range and occupation of the customers. List two other pieces of data about the customers that would be useful.

2 Explain why this sort of data is useful.

The marketing mix

- The marketing mix is the ingredients that businesses use to achieve marketing aims.

- A business may change its marketing strategy over time by altering its marketing mix.

A The 'four Ps' of the marketing mix

remember >>

Businesses place different emphasis on elements of the marketing mix.

>> **key fact** The marketing mix is made up of Product, Promotion, Price and Place.

A successful marketing mix of a good product in the right place at the right price, with attractive packaging and advertising, wins customers and makes profits more likely. Decisions have to be made about:

Product
- Quality: needs constant review.
- Range: develop new products, or concentrate on small number?
- After sales service: builds reputations and sales.
- Features and facilities: alterations/ updates can completely 'remake' a product.
- Size and packaging: may be crucial to customers.

Price
- Basic price level: needs constant review.
- Discounts: could win new customers.
- Pricing: varies for different customers.

The four Ps

Promotion
- Expenditure: how much?
- Style and substance: posters, adverts, local leafleting?
- Timing: regular, seasonal, aimed at particular time of day? Vital at launch of new product.
- Media: press, TV, point-of-sale, telephone, local or national?

Place
- Distribution: most common distribution chain is producer-wholesaler-retailer-customer, but shorter chains, e.g. producer-consumer, cut costs.
- Direct selling: home selling, mail order, TV and computer sales are all growing sectors of the market.
- Delivery and stock levels: sales lost if these areas are inefficient. Increase delivery fleet?

B The marketing strategy and marketing mix

In creating the marketing mix for a product, a business will concentrate on different elements from the lists opposite: the business will have an underlying strategy which depends on factors such as whether the product is new or the market highly competitive.

1 A business might have a strategy to set up a new product in an existing market. Because of a limited budget, the business uses low pricing, quick delivery and relies on word-of-mouth marketing.

2 If a business is trying to boost the sales of a well-established product, it may create new product features, improve the product quality, run a new advertising campaign or try to attract a new group of customers.

New technology has made a big difference to the marketing strategies of some businesses, e.g. bookshops. Internet sites allow access to customers worldwide. A marketing campaign to promote the website address, then a well-designed website backed by good customer service, should increase sales.

>> practice questions

A fast food chain is opening a new restaurant in a town centre. Marketing efforts will be aimed at raising awareness among local people. Future marketing will depend on the sales revenue from the restaurant. The budget is £10 000, and various methods could be used:

Large posters on key sites	*£400 per poster per month*
Local leaflets	*£175 per 10 000 leaflets*
Local newspaper adverts	*£550 per advert*
Local schools competition	*£500 for prizes*
Meal discount offers	*£2 per meal*
Radio adverts	*£300 per 30 seconds*

1 What methods would you use to promote the fast food restaurant and why?

2 Once the restaurant was open, what marketing mix could be used to ensure customers kept returning?

exam tip >>

You don't need to write about all the 'four Ps' in every answer. Choose only those most relevant to the situation.

The product life cycle

A The product life cycle

❶ key fact Products have a natural life cycle.

A product's life cycle begins with its development and launch, moves through a period of growth to maturity, then reaches a point where the market is full of similar competing products. Finally a loss of sales leads to the end of the cycle.

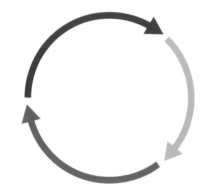

❷ key fact Forward-looking businesses constantly try to develop new and improved products.

- Product development may take a long time and be costly, especially where health and safety are important product features.

- The main elements in product development are: establishing customer needs; generating new ideas; checking production is viable and that the business can afford to go ahead; producing and testing prototypes; test marketing; developing a marketing strategy.

❸ key fact The stages of a product life cycle can be shown on a graph.

Hi-tech products (e.g. computers) tend to have short life cycles, as new developments quickly make old machines outdated. Standard essentials (e.g. salt) usually have long cycles.

Rapid growth is likely as the product gets established in the market.

A mature product is well set, but other similar products are now coming onto the scene. Without the same development costs, competitors are likely to be charging a lower price.

A saturated market has so many products that there is no longer room for growth.

When new products begin to appear, the original market goes into decline.

maturity

saturation

growth

decline

launch

SALES

TIME

remember >>

The graph shape will vary according to the product and length of its cycle.

62

B Extending the life cycle

>> **key fact** Businesses use many methods to try to extend product life cycles.

① However brilliant, a product unwanted by consumers will not sell. Other products may sell well for a while, then lose popularity. Firms spend lots of money on research and development before marketing a product, and on extending a product's life cycle once it is in the market.

② Life cycles can be lengthened by: extra advertising/promotion; new packaging (e.g. luxury versions); special deals; widening the product range (e.g. making DVDs of books); changing the product image to aim at a new market segment; diversifying a product (e.g. Mars ice cream bar).

C Branding

① Branding involves developing a product's name with a logo, colours and packaging, and registering it to stop other companies from using it.

② Branding helps preserve the life of a product by: making customers feel secure regarding quality; making it hard for new rivals to gain attention; making it simpler for customers to choose.

③ Strong branding is evident in the sweets market with some £126 million spent each year on advertising. A new brand can be a 'top twenty' selling sweet within a year or two, but big firms like Cadbury's have successfully maintained up to forty brand versions of chocolate.

④ Many high-street stores and supermarkets have copied the idea of branding for their own range of products. 'Own brands' now account for one third of sales in supermarkets.

⑤ Branding may not work where products are seen as essentially the same by consumers. Fresh fruit is an example, although Outspan and others have had some success.

⑥ A market leader's name is often used to refer to all products in the market (e.g. Biros, Hoovers).

remember >>

Fashions can repeat themselves. Yoyos have come back to life after decline on several occasions.

>> practice questions

Allsports manufactures high-quality sports and leisure shoes for specialist shops and department stores to sell under their own labels. It is now thinking of marketing its own brand label of sports shoes in this very competitive market.

1 What is meant by a 'very competitive market'? Use examples to illustrate your answer.

2 What problems might Allsports have in marketing its own brand label?

Pricing decisions

- The price of a product is determined by supply (from producers) and demand (of consumers).

- Businesses use different pricing policies to win or hold market share.

A Price, supply and demand

>> **key fact** The price that satisfies both business and customers will 'clear' the market.

In theory:

1 The higher the price of a product, the more a business will supply.

2 The higher the price, the less consumers will demand.

3 The ideal price is where supply and demand meet (the equilibrium price).

4 The equilibrium price satisfies both a business and its customers and the market will 'clear'.

5 Too low a price, and demand will outstrip supply. Too high a price, and there will be a surplus of unsold products.

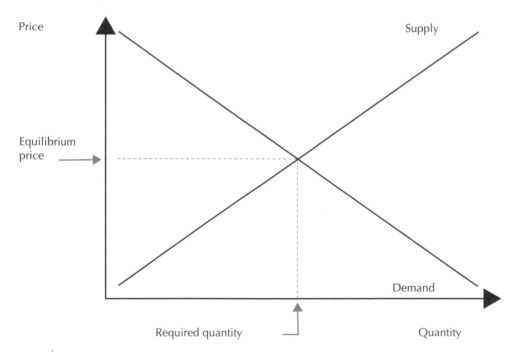

In practice, it is difficult to get information about all the decisions of businesses and consumers, so businesses set prices based on their objectives and 'best guesses' about the state of the market.

remember >>

A supply and demand diagram helps predict what will happen if demand is greater/less than supply.

B Pricing policies

>> **key fact** **Pricing is part of an overall marketing strategy used to persuade customers to buy a product.**

Prices must be monitored and adjusted when necessary to take account of such things as new competition, or rises and falls in demand.

1. **Cost-plus pricing**: a percentage mark-up is added to the total unit costs of production to give a business its profit margin. This takes no account of variations in fixed costs with output, or what customers will pay, but is a common approach.

    (A similar policy, **contribution pricing**, sets prices to cover variable costs and make a contribution towards fixed costs.)

2. **Competitive pricing**: a firm sets its price close to those of its rivals so competition effectively focuses on non-price features such as quality of service.

3. **Loss-leaders**: prices are set at or below cost in order to penetrate a new market. Supermarkets often use this approach, attracting customers to cheap goods on the basis that they will then buy other items. Penetration pricing is similar, with prices set above cost but below rivals.

4. **Skimming** (or **creaming**) **the market**: highlights a product's uniqueness, e.g. new hi-tech equipment is often given a high price as some people will buy it as a luxury. This enables development costs to be recovered. Later, the price can be dropped to attract a wider market.

5. **Price discrimination**: different prices are charged to different groups for the same product. Rail companies and airlines use this widely, e.g. some train passengers are charged a premium for rush hour travel while others can fill empty seats at a low price during off-peak times.

6. **Consumer-led pricing**: consumers develop a sense of a 'fair price', and products priced too far above or below this won't sell well, unless seen as true 'luxury' or 'bargain' products. This is known as a 'price plateau' and all businesses must be aware of it.

> **remember >>**
>
> **Pricing can be a matter of psychology. £1.99 feels a better price for some people than £2.00.**

>> practice questions

Fill-up Foods PLC make and sell snacks in a very competitive market. Research suggests a gap in the adult snacks market, but pricing will be vital. The marketing manager suggests prices should start low and then rise once brand loyalty is established.

1 **Explain what might happen to sales if Fill-up's price was higher than its competitors.**

2 **Suggest and explain alternative pricing policies that the company might use.**

> **exam tip >>**
>
> **Think about how the company can gain an edge over its rivals. Pricing policies will differ according to the level of competition.**

Promoting products

> Promotion is how a firm tells likely customers about a product and its benefits, in order to boost sales.

> It involves a mixture of information and persuasion and includes everything from advertising to free gifts.

A Promotion

>> **key fact** Promotion involves the way a product and its strengths are presented to consumers.

1. As part of its marketing strategy, a business may choose to spend more or less money on the promotion of a product at different stages in its life cycle.

2. A promotion campaign may be targeted at a national audience using every method available or may be a more local direct mailshot on a relatively small budget. It can set out to inform customers about the special features of a new product or try to persuade them that a product is better than others.

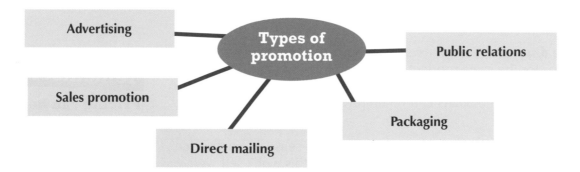

Advertising — Types of promotion — Public relations

Sales promotion — Packaging

Direct mailing

B Advertising

>> **key fact** Advertising is an important way of promoting a product.

1. Most companies use some form of advertising to promote their products. This can be through a variety of media, such as: TV, radio and cinema; newspapers and magazines; journals or specialist publications; posters on billboards.

2. Some types of advertising are more expensive than others, and are likely to reach many more people. Businesses spend over £15 billion on advertising in the UK. The largest part is spent on press and TV adverts.

3. Companies advertise: to persuade people to buy the product; to change people's attitudes; to make people think better of an organisation; to provide basic information.

remember >>

The Advertising Standards Authority (see page 71) makes sure advertising standards are kept high.

>> **key fact** Other forms of promotion can be short term (e.g. a one-off direct mailing) or part of a longer-term activity (e.g. a three-year sports sponsorship deal).

1 **Public relations** activities aim to keep a company's name in the public eye and ensure good customer relations. A public relations department is responsible for:

- press releases (e.g. about a new product)
- organising sponsorships and awards (e.g. for sports or educational activities)
- damage limitation – putting the company point of view in the event of unfavourable publicity.

2 **Sales promotion** activities include:

- special offers (buy two, get one free)
- price discounts
- vouchers, coupons and customer loyalty cards
- joint promotions (where one firm links to another, e.g. McDonald's and Disney)
- point-of-sale materials (displays and packaging in store)
- free gift campaigns or prize competitions (e.g. in children's book or toy shops).

3 **Direct mailing** ('junk mail'):

- involves sending promotional material to targeted customers
- uses databases of names built up from questionnaires, guarantee cards etc.
- is used to promote a variety of goods and services (e.g. book and music clubs, financial services, charity work).

4 **Packaging** often defines and identifies a product, and can be the most persuasive ingredient when consumers choose an item from the shelf.

- Good packaging must protect the product.
- It must be the right size and shape for easy use by distributors and customers.
- It must also have consumer appeal.
- Many large companies use professional design agencies to help them develop the most eye-catching look, and also to create seasonal looks, e.g. at Christmas.

>> practice questions

Fill-up Foods PLC hopes to sell more snacks in pubs, supermarkets and garages. What are the pros and cons of running a local TV advertising campaign to promote a new snack?

exam tip >>

Remember the pros and cons are with reference to other means of promotion.

The business environment

 The success of a business partly depends on external factors.

 Businesses face many risks and must plan for uncertainties as well as foreseeable events.

A External influences

>> **key fact** A business's success depends on external as well as internal influences.

Business rivals	Industry	Government
• can be a threat if their prices are lower • can help to boost trade for everyone	• may set guidelines, e.g. on pollution • may promote products for all businesses	• legislation may affect business costs • can help to raise business confidence

prices and quality to complete with

voluntary codes to abide by

laws to abide by, agencies to satisfy

Business

demands for choice and quality to fulfil

demands for good practice

overseas markets more accessible via the Internet

Customers	Pressure groups	Global economy
• consumer tastes may change • can stay loyal to a particular brand	• can be a threat if they gain publicity • can be a boost if products seen to be good	• ups and downs in trade • a slump in a big economy can affect everyone

B Planning for uncertainty

>> **key fact** The external business environment is full of risks. Good planning and government support can minimise the risks.

A number of external factors can create difficulties for a business. For instance:

- If the economic outlook is gloomy, a new business or product will be less likely to succeed.

- An unforeseen problem with a product may be discovered.

- Rival firms may use new technology to improve their products.

- Interest rates may rise, increasing the cost of loans.

- Exchange rates may change, making foreign trade more difficult.

Facing up to uncertainty and change

If just one store sold computers, it could set a high price. When many businesses are competing, expect lower prices, better service and lots of new products. **A business can monitor rivals when planning new products/marketing campaigns.**

Large out-of-town stores offer choice and cheaper prices to customers with cars and can benefit local communities. But there may be costs – town centre shops can lose customers and traffic may increase. **Government planning rules can help balance the interests of communities, small local businesses and big stores.**

Computer sales rely on good marketing and customers having money to spend. If unemployment rises and people cut back on spending, selling products will be more difficult. High interest rates make it hard for businesses to borrow funds for investment/product development. **The government's bank can help by managing interest rates. Businesses need to time any big loans carefully.**

A UK computer software business selling to the home market is likely to face competition from foreign firms. The business may also wish to sell abroad. Its prices may be lower than its rivals but a high UK exchange rate can make it hard to sell to other countries. Labour costs may be lower in other countries and a UK business may find it hard to compete. **The business may use new technology to keep costs down. Governments can help by managing exchange rates.**

>> practice questions

Identify three ways in which a government could help business activity in the UK.

exam tip >>

Use different examples of government support rather than similar schemes.

Business and competition

- Competition is usually good for businesses and customers but can lead to bad practices.

- There are laws to protect businesses and consumers.

A The importance of competition

>> **key fact** A business must work harder to win customers in a competitive market.

1. Competition creates choice for consumers and ensures businesses minimise costs and invest in developing new products. Businesses that cut corners to win customers may gain a bad reputation.

2. Businesses generally operate in competitive environments, for instance: where there are many rivals (e.g. town centre clothes shops); where customers have a wide choice of products (e.g. restaurants).

3. A business will generally do well if it: gives good personal service and is known to replace faulty products; has good marketing techniques; has competitive pricing; provides high levels of quality and standards; responds well to issues raised by pressure groups.

B Why businesses need controls

>> **key fact** Competition may lead to businesses behaving in unacceptable ways.

1. Businesses can exaggerate claims for their products.

2. Successful firms may charge very low prices to force rivals out of business.

3. When one firm dominates a market they may disregard customer views.

4. Some products may be profitable but undesirable (e.g. cigarettes, alcohol).

C Controls on businesses

>> **key fact** Business competition is regulated through various mechanisms.

Competition laws

UK and European Union laws stop businesses fixing prices or restricting supply. In Britain, the Competition Commission investigates cases where:

> **remember >>**
>
> Competition helps keep down costs but can lead to wasteful advertising.

- 25% or more of the market is in one business's hands
- a merger between businesses involves assets over £70 million.

Consumer laws

The three main laws protecting the consumer are:

- Trade Descriptions Act (1968, 1972): Stops firms giving misleading information.
- Consumer Credit Act 1974: Protection when borrowing or buying on credit.
- Sale and Supply of Goods Act 1994: Products have to be of 'satisfactory quality'.

Local government organisations

- Trading Standards Officers check on faulty products and weights and measures.
- Environmental Health Officers check on issues such as food hygiene and pollution.
- An Ombudsman checks public complaints, e.g. against government services.

Independent organisations

- The British Standards Institute (BSI) tests products for safety and quality and issues 'Kitemarks' to products that meet certain standards.
- Citizens Advice Bureaux provide free advice and help people to make complaints.
- The Office of Fair Trading provides information and advice leaflets.
- Agencies set up by the Government, e.g. OFTEL, OFGAS, check that private businesses don't abuse their monopoly position.

Voluntary codes

- Some industries have their own codes of conduct, e.g. the Association of British Travel Agents (ABTA) promises to get customers home from holiday if a firm goes bust.
- The Advertising Standards Authority (ASA) encourages advertisers to make 'legal, decent, honest and truthful' adverts.

>> practice questions

Baz reduces the price of some T-shirts in his shop. He labels each one to say it has faded after being on display. A customer buys one but returns it the next day demanding her money back.

1 Is the customer's complaint justified? Refer to relevant consumer protection laws.

2 State and explain one action Baz could take.

3 Suggest two organisations where the consumer could get advice.

4 What actions could these organisations take if the law had been broken?

exam tip >>

Learn the main two or three consumer protection laws and the key reason for each one.

Business and the community

> Businesses need good working relationships with their local community to operate successfully.

> Some costs and benefits of business activities may be felt by the wider community.

A Businesses need the goodwill of a local community

>> key fact A business needs the goodwill of a local community to survive long term.

A business may feel its main interest is in making a profit and that local community interests are not a priority. But a business needs:

1 **planning consent** to operate in a community – planning laws may be used against unpopular businesses

2 **transport facilities** and other services provided at a cost by the local community

3 **employees** and possibly emergency support from the local area.

B External costs and benefits

>> key fact Business activity has costs and benefits which are included in prices and profits. Other external costs and benefits felt by the community are not taken into account by individual firms.

External benefits add to the welfare of the community, but external costs cause problems. It can be difficult to get anyone to take responsibility for damage and hard to put a figure on the cost.

External benefits may include:

✔ **Improved transport and communications**; job gains (new employment and income); extra spending in local shops from those employed; **regeneration of local area** (new buildings, shops etc. because of new wealth); **efficient recycling** (some businesses use heat from waste burners as a power source).

External costs may include:

✘ **Pollution**; **safety hazards** from factories and traffic; **waste products for disposal** (general rubbish, smoke, gases, toxic substances); **building in rural areas** (damage to beauty spots and wildlife populations); **job losses** (unemployment from failure and closure of rival businesses); **lost income and spending power** of those unemployed; **loss of local services** (useful local buildings/services may be closed to make way for developments).

A proposal for an out-of-town shopping centre might attract support from those who consider more shops, jobs and a better image for the town as being of great benefit to the local community.

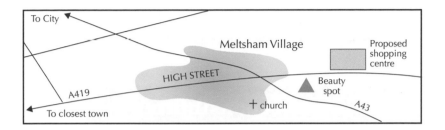

But there might be opposition too ...

C Balancing costs and benefits

>> **key fact**   It can be difficult to put a figure on external costs and benefits.

A business and its local community try to balance external costs and benefits, to arrive at a solution satisfactory to all. It can be difficult to put a figure on external costs and to persuade customers or business owners to pay for them (although some businesses, such as the Body Shop and BP, have begun to include costs of their activities to local communities in their balance sheets). However, if costs are looked at in terms of offsetting benefits, agreements may be reached.

For example:

1   Some businesses have replaced production techniques with versions that are more environmentally friendly (an external benefit), but customers have agreed to pay more for the products in return.

2   A community charges a company high business rates (local tax), but in return pays for the upkeep of the road, and the refuse-collection service to its out-of-town site.

3   The Government has begun to think about 'green taxes' to pay for external environmental costs – for example, charging businesses for the cost of maintaining roads used by fleets of lorries. A high licence fee can be charged for each lorry.

>> practice questions

A large leisure theme park is proposed for an area just outside a small town. A major road passes through the centre of the town and some people have long argued for a by-pass.

1 List some external benefits that the theme park might bring for the local community.

2 What might be some of the external costs?

3 How could these be paid for if the development went ahead?

Business ethics

➤ Businesses, like people, make choices about whether an activity is right or wrong (ethical).

➤ A strong ethical responsibility can be good for business.

A Different views of business responsibility

1 key fact Many businesses aim to behave responsibly as well as to make profits.

Some such businesses:

- help to pay for damage to the environment caused by their factories
- appoint directors with responsibility for ensuring 'fair pay' in the business
- agree to pay higher prices for raw materials as part of a 'fair trade' agreement.

2 key fact Many businesses argue that their job is to obey the law and make profits, no more.

Such businesses believe that:

- customers want cheap products, not Fairtrade products
- they must use the cheapest workers, even if jobs go in the area where the business began
- it's the government's job to look after the environment.

B The importance of business ethics

1 Customers: many customers need or want to know what has been used in the making of a product. Some businesses share more information about good/bad components or ingredients than others. In the long term, customers will buy from a business which they know trades fairly and honestly.

2 Workers: an ethical business will care about its staff and will often pay more than the going rate for the job. The business will provide training and allow for time off for parents to look after children.

3 Rival businesses: a business must decide what is acceptable in winning trade from rivals. Should a bus company push prices down so low that other, smaller business rivals go out of business? Should bribes be used to win overseas business?

4 Local communities: should businesses 'earn the right' to operate in a local community, for example by helping to support charitable activities or by sponsoring a new community building? Should a giant supermarket care about the small high-street shops threatened by its development?

⑤ **The environment**: some businesses change the landscape (e.g. a quarry); some cause pollution through waste products (e.g. power generation); some make products with hazardous materials (e.g. car battery manufacturers). Ethical businesses help to cover the environmental costs, but should they be leading new developments or just obeying laws at the least possible cost?

C Case study – Co-op

The Co-op has a strong ethical position.
Their website outlines some of the beliefs of the company:

combating climate change
We are amongst the world's leading businesses tackling climate change. We work in local communities through our Walking Buses scheme and Green Energy for Schools initiative.
more on climate change ▸

tackling global poverty
We help people in the developing world lift themselves out of poverty through our leading commitment to Fairtrade, charitable products, providing finance to the working poor and overseas projects.
more on global poverty ▸

inspiring young people
We believe in young people. That's why we're engaging more than 100,000 of them with our community projects this year, so that they can make a positive contribution to their communities.
more on young people ▸

other areas of social responsibility

assisting communities	launching unique ethical policies
find out more ▸	find out more ▸
improving animal welfare	RNID is our 2009 Charity of the Year
find out more ▸	find out more ▸
The Co-operative Community Plan	Sustainability Report 2007/08
find out more ▸	find out more ▸

>> practice questions

1 Using examples, explain two ways in which the Co-op claims to be acting in an ethically responsible way as a business.

2 What arguments could you use to persuade a shareholder interested mainly in profit, that a business should spend more on ethical activities?

The national economy

Governments try to manage the economy to provide stability for businesses.

They raise taxes to pay for different policies.

A How governments manage the economy

>> **key fact** Governments manage the economy to provide stability for businesses.

Business activity can be affected by government policies and the state of the national economy. Businesses expect governments to steer the economy towards steady growth and avoid sharp fluctuations in prices, interest rates and exchange rates.

In the UK, we also expect our government to: provide some goods and services for everyone; ensure the poorest are helped by the better-off (through taxes and benefits); keep price levels steady and encourage training and jobs.

The government uses different policies to affect the economy:

1 It taxes income, spending and business profits then uses the money for welfare benefits, services (e.g. health, education) and investment in new roads/buildings. Some of these policies are targeted at poorer regions of the country.

2 Tax and spending (fiscal policy) is managed through the yearly Budget.

3 The government's bank makes changes in interest rates (monetary policy) to encourage borrowing and investment by consumers and businesses.

B Managing the business cycle

>> **key fact** The government tries to smooth out big swings in the business cycle.

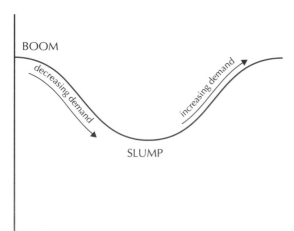

BOOM

decreasing demand

increasing demand

SLUMP

Growth in UK business output averages 2–3% a year but tends to fluctuate in cycles every 4–5 years. Growth and employment are helped by high demand in the economy. If demand outstrips supply, there can be a general increase in prices (inflation) and business planning becomes difficult.

If the government raises taxes, it can reduce demand but at the risk of pushing up unemployment and shaking business confidence.

remember >>

Governments can help but can't control all the factors that make business risky.

76

Falling demand affects:

Jobs: fewer goods bought by customers, falling sales, cut back on employment, business survival is more difficult

Trade: a worldwide fall in demand means less trade unless UK businesses keep prices below foreign competitors

Government finance: fewer sales and fewer jobs means less tax paid to government; unemployment means more government spending on support. This may result in budget problems and an increase in national debt.

C How a government raises and uses taxes

>> **key fact** Governments raise taxes in various ways from individuals and businesses to pay for different policies.

Income tax: the UK government takes 30–35% of pay through income tax and national insurance contributions. Currently, the basic rate of income tax is 20% for most workers. A higher rate leaves people with less income so discourages spending.

Value Added Tax (VAT): a tax on spending (17.5% on most goods and services; excludes essentials like children's clothes and basic food). A higher rate may discourage spending and push up prices.

Corporation tax: paid by companies on their income (profit). A rise in this tax could mean less investment and so cut future employment levels.

What does the government do with the money taken in taxes?

The money pays for education, health and other services as well as a wide range of welfare benefits. It also helps businesses through a variety of schemes:

1. **Assisted areas:** grants given to businesses who set up within a designated area.

2. **Inner cities:** development corporations take over a whole area that has declined, rebuild the infrastructure and oversee private sector investment in the area.

3. **Enterprise zones:** business spending on new buildings is not taxed in these areas and businesses do not have to pay business rates for a period of time.

4. **Small businesses:** given help with loans and start-ups.

The European Union also provides grants and has Enterprise Zone schemes. Local Councils help to put national schemes into practice in the local area.

>> practice questions

A Canadian Company, Carco, wants to open a factory in Kirston, a UK town in decline since the closure of a major industrial plant. The local council has worked hard to improve roads and subsidise a new industrial estate, which has been designated as an Enterprise Zone.

1 Kirston Business Park is an Enterprise Zone. What does this mean to Carco?

2 How else will Carco benefit from setting up in Kirston?

3 Why is the arrival of Carco important for the region and for the economy?

exam tip >>

Avoid phrases like 'they can do this' when writing about government activity. Be specific: refer to the government or local councils as appropriate.

Business and Europe

- The European Union (EU) provides a common trading area for 27 countries.

- The euro is a common currency used by most EU members, but not currently the UK.

A The EU as a common trading area

>> **key fact** The EU provides a common trading area which offers many shared benefits.

1. UK businesses operate in a combined EU market of some 500 million people.

2. The EU has regulations, policies and guidelines which help and control business activity.

3. Over 58% of the UK's overseas trade is with other EU countries.

4. The EU aims to achieve social and economic progress for its members through economic growth and expansion of trade.

5. The EU Budget is financed by contributions from member states and from tariffs (taxes charged) on imports from outside the EU.

6. EU membership may continue to expand as further European countries join.

Benefits of EU membership

Better protection
- The Social Chapter sets out rights and regulations for the workplace.
- Consumer rights are protected throughout the EU; free competition is upheld.

Support
- Aid is directed at poorer regions, including parts of the UK.
- The Common Agricultural Policy helps create security for farmers by buying produce at guaranteed prices. The EU also provides grants to modernise farms.

Easier trade
- People and goods can travel freely across member countries.
- VAT has been harmonised – it cannot fall below 15% in any EU country.
- People can seek jobs throughout the EU.

Environmental standards
- The Common Fisheries Policy controls the amount of fish that countries or individual fishermen can catch.
- Environmental standards (often stricter than British laws) are set for all members.

remember >>

Think how European membership affects UK businesses.

B The euro as a single currency

 >> key fact **The euro has become a common currency for most EU members but is still being debated in the UK.**

In 2002, the euro became the single currency for most EU member countries. A European central bank supports the system and each country has to keep its economy under strict control.

The UK has not yet joined the single currency.

Advantages	<ul><li>Businesses no longer have to pay a fee to change their money when selling or buying from other countries.</li><li>Businesses no longer need to worry about exchange rate fluctuations when trading across Europe.</li><li>The European Central Bank can make long-term decisions for the benefit of the whole of Europe.</li></ul>
Disadvantages ✖	<ul><li>Individual countries lose direct control over their economy. A decision which benefits Europe may not be good for an individual country.</li><li>Each country has to abide by tight economic guidelines. This may result in higher unemployment, extra taxes and fewer choices for the government.</li></ul>

>> practice questions

One of the best-known features of the EU is the single market.

1 What is meant by a single market?

2 How does a single market help member countries trade in the EU?

3 Why does the single market persuade foreign firms to set up factories in the EU?

exam tip >>

Show that you know there are different views on the euro and EU membership, using phrases like 'from a large business point of view'.

The global economy

- UK businesses compete for world markets.
- Changes in the value of the pound affect British firms.
- Governments try to boost exports and limit imports.

A UK businesses and world markets

>> **key fact** UK traders face stiff competition in world markets.

Firms selling goods abroad have to compete in worldwide markets, but doing so successfully gives a country the revenue to buy specialist or cheap goods from abroad.

International trade means:

✔ larger markets and lower costs; more opportunities to boost sales; more consumers with diverse tastes.

But it also means:

✘ greater distances for deliveries; customs taxes, paperwork and delays at international borders; the need for different currencies; promotional materials in various languages; different laws and customs to deal with.

remember >>

International companies may market the same product in many different countries.

B The importance of exchange rates

>> **key fact** Exchange rate fluctuations affect British firms which trade abroad.

- The value of one currency against another is called its exchange rate.

- UK businesses need foreign currency to trade abroad. Foreign businesses need pounds to buy British goods or invest in British companies.

- As in any other market, increased demand for pounds will push up its 'price'. This affects the price of exports and imports. Frequent changes in the exchange rate create uncertainty for businesses.

- Governments try to keep the exchange rate stable. If there is pressure on the pound because of high demand, the government can supply extra currency from its reserves.

C Government action to promote trade

① key fact
The government tries to help UK businesses by boosting exports and restricting imports.

- **Imports** are goods and services bought from abroad with payments flowing out to foreign producers.

- UK producers sell **exports** abroad and the money earned comes back into the UK.

- These flows of money are recorded on the country's **balance of payments**.

- The UK usually imports more than it exports. The country has a surplus on trade in services, but a big deficit on trade in goods which means there is an overall **trade deficit**.

To improve the situation, businesses need to make goods and services more competitive, for instance by investing in training and new technology.

② key fact
A number of government measures can be used to reduce a trade deficit.

- Tariffs (taxes) on imports increase their price and encourage consumers to buy home produce.

- No taxes on exports allows businesses to be competitive in overseas markets.

- Advice to businesses on selling in overseas markets.

- Import quotas restrict imports into the country. Such a policy may lead to retaliatory bans.

- Subsidies provide businesses with government money to help keep down their costs and so enable them to charge lower prices than rivals in other countries.

- Exchange control restricts access to foreign currency, making importing and travel more difficult.

- Government advertising campaigns can encourage people to buy home-produced goods and services, while running trade fairs abroad can boost exports.

>> practice questions

Jo runs a craft centre and restaurant near a major tourist attraction in Yorkshire. She expects trade from foreign tourists, especially the Japanese, to increase by 10% in the next six months and by up to 30% in the next year. She is thinking of extending her restaurant.

1 How might Jo's business be affected by:
   a) a decrease in the value of the pound against the yen?
   b) a slump in the Japanese economy?

2 What could the government do to help Jo's business in the long term?

exam tip >>

When economic indicators go down, it isn't all bad news. What effects will there be on the costs of imports and exports? Think of the knock-on effects.

Exam questions and model answers

>> Specimen question 1

Jon and Michaela run a group of four fish restaurants called 'The Plaice' in the West of England.

The restaurants have a good reputation for using high-quality food and special customer service. Staff are well trained and have been loyal to the business. Jon and Michaela would like to grow their business and are considering selling 'The Plaice' franchises to people who want to start up a restaurant elsewhere.

a)   What is meant by a franchise? **2 marks**

b)   Give two reasons why someone might buy a franchise from Jon and Michaela. **5 marks**

c)   Jon and Michaela are thinking of paying staff higher than average wages. Do you think this is the best way of motivating their staff? Give reasons. **9 marks**

>> Model answer 1

a)   When a business allows others to use its products or brand in return for a regular payment or share of profits.

b)   Makes it easier to start up a business when you use a known 'brand', less risk.
Can use expertise of others to help provide marketing and suppliers.

Note that to score full marks, the answer must be written from the point of view of the franchisee, not franchiser.

c)   Best way given that most people are motivated by money, catering industry well-known for low pay, but Maslow suggests valuing people as people, not just money, so responsibility may matter as well. Higher wages increases costs and this may not help the business at this point. On balance, higher wages are a good idea but may be more of a short term solution.

Note that to score good marks, several reasons should be considered, points should be considered 'for' as well as 'against', and a judgement should be made, at the end, with a reason why it seems the best decision. (In this case, OK for a short time but not the best way of motivating in the longer term.)

>> Specimen question 2

Provost PLC makes animal feed and is in competition with many small businesses operating as sole traders.

a)   How might Provost PLC differ from sole traders in the following ways:

   i)   Ownership? **2 marks**

   ii) Where to obtain finance to set up the business? **4 marks**

   iii) Distribution of profits? **2 marks**

b)   State two major business objectives Provost PLC might have and explain why they are important to the company. **4 marks**

>> Model answer 2

a)   **i)** Provost will be owned by its many shareholders. These are members of the public who had the cash to buy the shares when they were offered for sale. A sole trader is owned just by the person who set up the business.

It gives an accurate description of the ownership of both a PLC and a sole trader. It makes it clear that, with a PLC, it is ownership of shares which gives part ownership of the company. The number of owners is important because it will change the way decisions are made.

ii) Both Provost and a sole trader could finance their business from the owners' funds, but because there may be thousands of shareholders, Provost could raise a larger sum. It could raise further funds by issuing new shares. Provost is a large company and so is likely to borrow larger sums from the bank. The bank can be more certain of getting its money back. Provost may already have assets like a factory, which it could sell and lease back to raise funds.

The answer concentrates on Provost but makes it clear that it is comparing this with a sole trader. The first section deals with two aspects of finance through shares and is worth two marks. It appears first and is given more importance.

The two other points are made simply and clearly.

There is no need to repeat this for the sole trader.

iii) Shareholders can be paid some of the profits as an annual dividend but Provost's managing board will have to decide if there are enough profits available. These profits may be put back into the business. Different shareholders with different kinds of shares can be given first share of the profits.

The sole trader decides on keeping the profits or putting them into the business.

This answer is clear on who decides and who gets the benefit in the two different businesses.

b)   **To make profits**: An important business objective as it is usually the overriding reason why people work or invest.

To produce a safe and high quality product: An animal feed business needs to be safe, especially after the BSE scare. A quality product will ensure future buyers.

The business objectives have been linked to Provost's products.

Simple explanations have been used which remind us of some of the different stakeholders.

>> Further questions

1   The following are features of different kinds of business organisations:

   • Between two and twenty owners

   • Owners have limited liability

   • Issues shares

   • Owners usually have unlimited liability

   a) Which two are features of a partnership? **2 marks**

   b) Which two are features of a private limited company? **2 marks**

   c) What is meant by limited liability? **2 marks**

2   A sportswear company has a good market share and is competing with foreign firms. The managers believe there is little scope for internal growth and are seeking a merger with another company.

   What are the advantages of growing through a merger rather than by internal growth? **5 marks**

Business production

>> Specimen question

Goodwood Ltd makes wooden garden items (sheds, tables and chairs, bird tables and fence panels). These are sold in the factory shop and in garden centres all over England. The company also builds special 'one-off' items at the request of customers.

a) The 'one-off' items are made using 'job production'. State and explain two features of job production. **6 marks**

b) i) Give one reason why job production is NOT suitable for the normal garden items. **2 marks**

   ii) What might be a better method of production for the normal garden items? Why? **6 marks**

c) In November, Goodwood get a new contract from a mail order company for the following:

   - 2000 sheds by August

   - 4000 tables by March

   - 16 000 chairs by March.

   Explain how completing the contract would affect production methods and use of labour. **4 marks**

>> Model answer

a) Skilled labour is used because each job requires something different. Each customer wants a different style of chair or table. The job is likely to take longer than making lots of similar items.

The answer is to the point and linked to the business of garden furniture.

b) i) Job production would not be suitable because large amounts of the same item are wanted.

   ii) Batch or mass production would be better because they can use machinery and repeat designs. Workers can train to do a particular job quickly.

Clear application of the advantages of batch/mass production to the business context.

c) The contract requires large numbers of similar products. Goodwood needs to switch most workers to batch production. Lots of workers are needed for March but fewer after that, so the business will probably employ workers on a temporary contract.

Good explanation of the consequences of the contract, viewed in two stages: November to March and March to August.

>> Further questions

1 Kitchen Designs PLC makes kitchen units for sale in a range of different designs.

   a) Explain fully how automating the process of production might help the firm. **4 marks**

   b) Interest rates in the UK have fallen to extremely low levels. Explain two ways in which a fall in interest rates might help Kitchen Designs PLC. **2 x 5 marks**

2 An international bridge-building company has, in the past, used expensive models to calculate the size and specification of its bridges using its own highly-trained engineers.

   a) What might be the advantages to this company of using the Internet to find suppliers? **4 marks**

   b) Explain how CAD could help the company in designing a new bridge. **4 marks**

   c) Suggest two problems the company might have in dealing with clients in remote parts of the world and how these problems could be overcome. **4 marks**

Business finance

>> Specimen question 1

Study the balance sheet for the company Property Ltd.

a) Fill in the missing figures for working capital and loans. Show your working out. **4 marks**

b) Give one example of a fixed asset and one of a current liability. **2 marks**

c) Explain the purpose of a balance sheet. **6 marks**

d) Explain the purpose of a profit and loss account. **6 marks**

>> Model answer 1

a) Working capital is the amount of capital available to pay immediate debts. This is current assets – current liabilities = £100 000 – £75 000 = £25 000.

Loans + retained profit + share capital = capital employed. Loans + £60 000 + £50 000 = £165 000. Loans = £55 000.

The answer shows understanding of key words (1 mark) and identifies correct items from the balance sheet (1 mark). It uses correct units (1 mark) and the calculation is correct (1 mark).

b) Fixed assets are things like equipment. Current liabilities are short-term debts like a bank loan.

c) It shows the financial position of a business at a particular moment. It shows all the liabilities on one side balanced by the assets on the other. It contains important information like the business's ability to pay its debts. This is important to anyone who lends money to the business.

This explanation gives an accurate description, shows some of the key ingredients and explains why they are important.

d) A profit and loss account shows the net profit and is usually published every 6 or 12 months. The total of expenses, losses and overheads are deducted from the sales revenue. A business can check its progress from this account, for example by comparing profits from one year with another, or comparing profits to the volume of sales.

Again, the key ingredients are mentioned and an example is given of how useful the figures may be in comparing profitability.

>> Specimen question 2

The finance director at TM Sportswear Ltd has drawn up a cash flow forecast (see overleaf) for next year's trading.

Sales at TM Sportswear Ltd for April to June totalled only £360 000 and the directors decide to take out an overdraft to solve this problem.

a) Advise the directors of TM Sportswear Ltd on the amount which should be borrowed and state the reason for your advice. **5 marks**

b) Shortly after taking out an overdraft, the interest rates of all banks increased. Explain how this will be a constraint to TM Sportswear Ltd. **5 marks**

Property Ltd
Balance sheet as at March 31st of current year

	£000	£000
Fixed assets		140
Current assets		
Stock	40	
Debtors	10	
Cash	50	
	100	
Current liabilities	75	
Working capital	?	
Net assets employed		**165**
Share capital	50	
Retained profit	60	
Loans (long-term)	?	
Capital employed		**165**

Cash flow forecast for TM Sportswear Ltd (£000)	Jan–Mar	Apr–Jun	Jul–Sep	Oct–Dec
	(£000)	(£000)	(£000)	(£000)
Receipts				
Sales	400	500	550	550
Total income	400	500	550	550
Payments				
Suppliers	250	250	275	275
Wages	15	15	15	15
Overheads	120	120	120	120
Total expenditure	385	385	410	410
Net cash flow	15	115	140	140
Opening balance	0	15	130	270
Closing balance	15	130	270	410

>> Model answer 2

a) TM Sportswear Ltd should borrow at least £125 000 because there will be a £25 000 shortfall for April–June if all the costings are accurate and there may be a shortfall of £50 000 per period for July–December if the pattern of poorer sales continues. It is possible that sales will pick up nearer Christmas but it is better to be safe than sorry.

The figures are accurate and show an understanding of how a problem may arise during this period and continue in the periods ahead. It makes good use of the case study in the reference to Christmas sales.

b) An increase in interest rates will push up the cost of the loan unless it was agreed at a fixed rate. The bank will expect to receive the interest payment and this may mean a greater cash loss and the business may have to find ways of cutting other costs.

This shows a clear understanding between interest rate changes and the cost of borrowing. It also provides an example of how the business might take action.

>> Further questions

1 T-pots Ltd plans to produce 8000 special teapots. It has estimated costs as shown in the chart:

   a) Give two examples of fixed costs. **2 marks**

   b) How does a fixed cost differ from a variable cost? **2 marks**

   c) Calculate the total cost of making each teapot. Show your working. **2 marks**

   d) If each teapot sells for £40, how much profit will be made if all 8000 teapots are sold? Show your working. **4 marks**

Fixed costs:	**£60 000**
Variable costs:	
labour	£145 000
raw materials	£38 000
power	£15 000
promotion	£20 000
other expenses	£10 000
	£228 000
Total costs:	**£288 000**

2 Lena opened an office two years ago and had enough work to employ an assistant. She now has one-year contracts with two large local firms and has had to move to new premises. She has taken on three new employees but has not enough cash to buy computers and office equipment. She is considering leasing the equipment or buying them on Hire Purchase.

a) Describe two features of leasing and two of Hire Purchase. **4 marks**

b) Which method of obtaining the equipment would you recommend and why? **6 marks**

People in business

>> Specimen question

Some employees have suggested to their manager that less money should be spent on staff training and on bonuses, and that the saving from this should be used to increase hourly pay rates.

a) Do you think all staff would benefit to the same degree from a general pay rise? **4 marks**

b) Why might this change damage worker motivation? **4 marks**

c) How might the employer gain or lose? **4 marks**

>> Model answer

a) If everyone was working in a similar way on similar jobs, then a general pay rise would be OK. But in many businesses, some workers put in overtime or can work faster for bonuses. They would lose out.

The writer shows that there is not a right or wrong answer. It depends on how the business production is organised. The meaning of bonus and hourly pay rate is understood.

b) Some workers would feel their extra effort is not valued and so not try so hard.
Some workers might feel the situation benefits others more than them.
Some workers may depend on training for promotion.

The importance of motivation is made clear and it is understood that good effort depends both on the worker and manager. The writer also understands the importance of training to workers.

c) Basic hourly pay rates are lower than bonuses and overtime. It might cut labour costs and more production might get done in planned working hours. Workers who don't get trained might produce poor work or might leave.

This shows good understanding of the changes from a business manager's perspective. It makes a connection between cause and effect.

>> Further questions

1   Jean runs her own clothes design business but needs to appoint an office manager to help run the business.

   a) State and explain three duties which the office manager might carry out. **6 marks**

   b) State and explain the sequence of events that would lead to the appointment of the office manager. **6 marks**

   c) The office manager will be responsible for induction training. How might induction training benefit the business and new employees? **8 marks**

2   A production manager at a sports goods factory feels the current production line will not cope with an increased range of higher quality products required by customers. He feels this is a good time to update the production process using teamwork and a 'Just-in-time' (JIT) system of stock control.

   a) Explain how the introduction of teamwork might affect the performance of the business. **6 marks**

   b) Examine the advantages and disadvantages of introducing a JIT system. **9 marks**

>> Specimen question 1

Goodwood Ltd makes wooden garden items (sheds, tables and chairs, bird tables and fence panels). These are sold in the factory shop and in garden centres all over England. The company also builds special 'one-off' items at the request of customers and has recently completed a large order for thousands of garden sheds, tables and chairs from a mail order company. Goodwood Ltd has decided to stop making chairs and tables out of wood but to make them from plastic instead.

Describe the sales promotion and advertising that should be undertaken in the short term. **8 marks**

>> Model answer 1

Goodwood Ltd may lose customers who prefer traditional wooden furniture. The company should promote the new plastic items at the point-of-sale in garden centres and send brochures to other mail order companies to win new orders. They might even choose to run an advert in a national newspaper with links to the various garden centres.

The advert could show a typical family enjoying the furniture in the garden and appeal to fun-loving families as well as those who like tasteful garden furniture.

It gives a reason why promotion is necessary (2 marks). It gives several different suggestions for the campaign (2 marks each) and refers to a typical target audience.

>> Specimen question 2

Many supermarkets stock their shelves with own brand products which sit alongside other well-known brands of goods.

a) Using two examples, explain what is meant by the term 'brand'. **4 marks**

b) Why do you think supermarkets sell their own brand label products as well as branded goods? **4 marks**

c) Outline and explain a strategy that a national supermarket chain might use to compete with its main rivals. **6 marks**

>> Model answer 2

a) A brand is the name given to a product to make it appear different to rivals. Timotei shampoo and Kellogg's Corn Flakes are examples.

Accurate explanation with relevant examples.

b) Own brands can help a supermarket capture market share and improve the firm's image. They also allow supermarkets to compete with each other and may help to increase company profits.

Four points are included in this tightly packed answer. An example might have been included.

c) A supermarket might run a loss-leading campaign with low prices on a few key products to win customers. They might then sell extra numbers of other goods. The supermarket could also offer loyalty cards with bonuses if the customers keep coming back to the store. A store might also offer to deliver goods locally which have been ordered over the Internet.

This answer has three different examples which fit into a sensible strategy to win customers from other supermarkets. Each suggestion has an example of how it might affect customers.

>> Further questions

1   Elegant Kitchens PLC intends to try to increase the sales of its 'Farmhouse' range of kitchen units by marketing it to middle and lower income groups.

   a)   Name four elements of the marketing mix.   **4 marks**

   b)   Suggest a marketing strategy which might be used by Elegant Kitchens PLC to increase sales of the 'Farmhouse' range to the middle and lower income groups.   **8 marks**

2   A business manager decides to use market research before trying to expand the business.

   a)   What is market research?   **3 marks**

   b)   How might the market research be carried out?   **3 marks**

   c)   Why does market research sometimes fail?   **4 marks**

The business environment

>> Specimen question

Many products are advertised as being 'environmentally friendly'. Some of these same products are sold in elaborate packaging. Claims made by businesses for their products have not always been checked out.

a)   Explain two ways in which a product could be 'environmentally friendly'.   **4 marks**

b)   Why do firms often use large amounts of resources in packaging products?   **4 marks**

c)   What are the costs to society of using resources for packaging?   **4 marks**

d)   Why might the government and the European Union pass laws to protect the consumer?   **6 marks**

>> Model answer

a)   Two points could be chosen from: recyclable, not tested on animals, efficient production, no dangerous materials.

Each relevant point needs to be linked to the idea of 'environmentally friendly'.

b)   Firms use lots of resources on packaging because it can improve the quality of the product, especially if freshness is important. The packaging can make the product stand out from other similar products. It may also be necessary to package some products safely, such as a kitchen knife.

This answer provides a good explanation of why packaging may be used, and makes use of examples.

c)   Lots of plastic packaging can add to problems of waste disposal and pollution. The materials may also be made from non-renewable resources and of course the resources could be used for something else. There is an opportunity cost.

Simple examples are given and the use of specialist terms strengthens the answer.

d)   The government could pass laws to make companies protect the environment and to provide better information on the labels explaining how care is being taken in the production of the product. Some businesses may spend more money than others and find it harder to compete. Therefore laws can provide a 'level playing field' for everyone.

Examples of government laws are mentioned with reasons as to how they might help.

>> Further question

1   Explain the advantages and disadvantages to a large UK transport company of membership of the European Union.   **10 marks**

Answers to further exam questions

Business types and objectives (page 83)

1 a) Between two and twenty owners; Owners usually have unlimited liability.

b) Issues shares; Owners have limited liability.

c) Owners risk losing only the value of the shares they bought, not all of their other assets.

2 A merger can take place quickly and can bring together the strengths of two businesses. It can give this company very quick access to other markets through the merged company and does not have to cost a lot of money. It can also spread the risk of business between the two companies.

Business production (page 84)

1 a) Machinery could be used to make standard kitchen units to a high standard. The machinery would initially cost a lot but could then work 24 hours a day and be very productive. Machinery would probably be quicker than humans. Orders could also be made to suit customers. Computer controls will help to spot breakdowns and should be very efficient.

b) If Kitchen Designs PLC has taken out a loan, it means it could afford to borrow more as the cost of repayments will be lower. This would mean that the company could afford to invest more in machinery and expand the company with confidence. A fall in interest rates may also encourage consumers to borrow and spend more knowing that their credit card repayments might also fall a little. They might pay for larger items like a new house or a new kitchen rather than put it off for better times. This would mean more business for the company.

2 a) It could find a supplier who provides materials at a lower cost, or who has a good reputation. It could search worldwide for such a supplier and, with more competition, the business should get a good deal.

b) The computer allows the engineers to build virtual models and try them out with sophisticated tests. This saves the time and money involved in building actual models, although training the engineers to use the software will require an initial investment. The company should be able to adjust the programme to any design.

c) The company representatives wouldn't meet the clients face to face and might not understand all of their needs without site visits. This may mean it is difficult to form a close and trusting relationship. There may need to be a lot of information exchanged. E-mail and video-conferencing would help this process as well as visits.

Business finance (page 86)

1 a) Fixed costs can be the cost of hiring or buying a factory, and the equipment which goes into it.

b) Variable costs change as more goods are produced; fixed costs stay the same even if there is no production at all.

c) TC = FC + VC = £60 000 + £145 000 + £38 000 + £15 000 + £20 000 + £10 000 = £288 000.

d) TR = £8000 @ £40 = £320 000;
Profit = TR-TC = £320 000 − £288 000 = £32 000.

2 a) Leasing means 'borrowing' the computers in return for a fee. The computers would be maintained by the business who leases them to Lena. If Lena uses hire purchase, she is buying the computers over a period of time. A finance company will lend the money and Lena will take ownership when she has paid back a certain percentage. She will pay more than a straight purchase but the computers will be available immediately.

b) Leasing may be the better option because she is not certain to keep the contracts for the business in a year's time and may have to 'downsize' again. If she does need to expand, or to update the computers, she can renegotiate the terms of the lease.

People in business (page 87)

1 a) Oversee all the paperwork, which might include liaising with customers outside of the business; manage the office and link with other managers in the business; take responsibility for the finances, including the day to day documentation and drawing up accounts at the end of the year.

b) There would need to be a job and a person specification drawn up with the help of other key staff. The job would have to be advertised in appropriate places, like fashion magazines, and a shortlist for interview drawn up. Candidates may be given a test to show they can manage an office and business links. The most suitable candidate would be offered the job, once references had been checked. Some training and an introductory period would be set to make sure everyone is happy.

c) Induction training makes sure all new staff understand their roles and what is expected of them. This avoids silly mistakes which could lose customers and also helps the new person to fit in. The training may motivate the new person and encourage them to stay. They pick up new skills and the company gets a good worker and a reputation as a good employer. In-house training is probably better than off-the-job training for this task.

2 a) Once a team is established, it is likely to encourage better work and increase motivation among staff. A team can support each other and may solve small problems without any breaks in production. The team may become multi-skilled and work on a more flexible basis. On the other hand, it will take time to establish and may not suit all workers. There will also be training costs.

b) A JIT system will mean that raw materials and parts arrive just in time for assembly purposes and the factory will not be cluttered with unnecessary piles of material. This should cut costs provided everything comes in on time. On the downside, it will require very reliable suppliers who know the business well and can deliver to time. If not, the sports factory will be at a standstill and customers will experience delays. Computers can help with communication and stock records ensuring that the system is not hard to support.

Business and marketing (page 89)

1 a) Price, promotion, product and place.

b) They could use a competitive pricing strategy, or perhaps even a cut price strategy, to gain the attention of their target market. They could also research what kind of kitchen units this particular group likes and target production to meet these needs. Advertisements in the magazines read by such customers, offering a special price for those who place an order by a certain date, could also help. This would give the business a good start. It may wish to sell through DIY outlets which could give the units a good display and suggest high quality.

2 a) Market research describes the methods used by a business to find out what customers' needs are and what products they prefer. It may also provide an insight into competitor activity.

b) Research could be desk-based using published secondary data. This approach is good when there are lots of trade publications and statistics collected on the particular product and market. Otherwise, surveys may have to be carried out by direct questionnaires, post or telephone. Researchers will be paid to collect and process this primary data.

c) Market research sometimes fails because the wrong questions are asked or because the information collected is incomplete or done in a hurry. There may not be a big enough source of finance to pay for the expensive collection of new data. If the product is very new, there are likely to be risks because no-one is sure they want the product. The failure in 2009 of Setanta Sports GB is a good example.

The business environment (page 89)

1 The EU can offer many advantages to a transport firm because they have to cross a lot of international boundaries to carry out their business. There would be no delays while frontier checks were made across the EU borders. The common currency and simplified paperwork with common rules should make most business deals easier to manage. Fuel prices and taxes should be roughly the same and so competition between European firms is fair. The EU would make sure that no other company behaved unfairly.

But the company would have to make sure they meet all the rules themselves and there are a lot of checks regarding transport vehicles. There are also rules about distances to travel and, of course, while EU doors are open to a UK firm, so too UK doors are now open to all sorts of competing firms. The EU has rules about employment and it may mean the UK firm has to change the way some drivers are employed. The UK has not yet joined the common currency, the Euro, so other European drivers may have an advantage with few currency problems. At the moment, taxes on fuel and roads are different between countries, so it may be difficult to compete in the short term.

Answers to practice questions

Business types (page 3)

1 **a)** Secondary
   b) Primary
   c) Tertiary
   d) Tertiary

2 Help to sell the cars, provide finance for researching new cars, help develop website for car customers

Enterprise and business planning (page 5)

1 You would expect to see details of how they've costed the equipment and their own costs, how they've forecast sales revenue and break even, and how much of the loan they plan to repay each year. You would also require clear agreement about how much interest and repayment will take place each year, the finishing date for repayments and guarantees for the money if the business has difficulties.

2 Product-driven firms are trying to force a product onto customers which they may not want, whereas a market-driven firm is responding to identified wants or needs.

Business objectives (page 7)

1 It will help the firm to grow, spread risks of trading in the north and could boost their own success.

2 Business owners' main interest is their reward for investment, the dividend payout which is their share of profits.

3 Customers in the south will have a new choice of products; customers in the north might not get as good a service if the business spends more attention on the launch in the south.

4 Managers might say that everyone's interest is in profit and that, in the years ahead, more profit might be earned from the expansion, even if the dividends are low to start with.

Business location (page 9)

1 Climate; close proximity to a large number of customers; other nearby leisure facilities

2 Climate first because many activities in an outdoor theme park require good weather to be safe and to be enjoyable. The number of customers comes next; if there are enough, it doesn't matter if there are rival attractions. Rival attractions will bring in customers to the area; they may then use the theme park.

Sole traders and partnerships (page 11)

1 **a)** John could lose all his assets, including his house, if the business went bust.

   b) John and his friend are joint owners of the business and are both liable for any debts.

2 **a)** You make all the decisions, keep all the profits and have the satisfaction of doing things your own way.

   b) The owners haven't planned the finances carefully enough; the business isn't successfully managed; the marketing is poor, or the products are not popular.

Growing a business (page 13)

1 Horizontal: e.g. another smoothie manufacturer; backward vertical: e.g. a fruit farm; forward vertical: e.g. a smoothie seller; diversification: e.g. a plumbing firm

2 Stead's Smoothies could take over another smoothie manufacturer, this would increase their market share in an area in which they specialise. They could take over a fruit farm, securing the provision of high quality raw materials. They could take over a smoothie seller as this would provide a guaranteed outlet for their products. They could take-over a plumbing firm as this would spread their risk in the event of their smoothie company struggling.

   In conclusion: take over the fruit farm as this will ensure they have a secure provision of raw materials which is important for a firm producing high quality goods.

Ltd companies and PLCs (page 15)

1 Limited liability

2 Shares are owned by friends and family of the original owner; shareholders are likely to share all of the business objectives.

3 If the business goes bust, the Greens will lose only the amount they own in shares.

4 They want to keep close control over the business; if they went PLC, anyone could buy shares and influence the decisions of the company.

Co-operatives and franchises (page 17)

1 Mike and Alan would benefit from the larger firm's name and marketing, as well as their trading expertise. They might also get help with the costs of renting a larger store.

2 The franchiser will expect an annual fee or even a share of any profits which they earn. They might also have to trade in a particular way demanded by the franchiser. They 'lose control' of parts of the business.

The public sector (page 19)

1 Privatisation means the selling of public sector organisations to the private sector.

2 **a)** The business might now be run more for profit and the interests of shareholders, rather than the interests of the customers and the community.

b) The quality of products might improve if the private firm decided to put more money into research and development. The quality might get worse if competition led to businesses cutting corners or only running profitable parts of the business.

c) Privatisation can lead to more competition if other businesses decide to enter the market; prices might then go down. If the business stays in one private company's hands, prices might rise as there is no control over a monopoly business.

Business organisation (page 21)

1

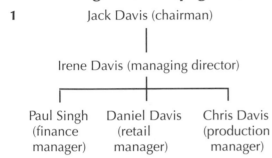

2 Division of labour means each employee specialising on one part of the production process.

3 Human resource management, distribution, research and development

4 Chain of command means the line of responsibility for decisions; span of control refers to the range of responsibility for any one person or department.

5 Accounts manager, payroll supervisor

6 Advantages: clear line of responsibility; opportunities for promotion

Disadvantages: decisions can take time to pass on; hard for people at the top and bottom to know what the other is doing

Business production (page 23)

1 Star: seasonal fruit; cash cow: bread; question marks: multicultural dinner kits; dogs: outdated electrical equipment

2 Supermarkets can use large warehouses to supply their own stores (technical economies). Products can be bought in large quantities straight from the supplier (trading economies). Specialist managers can be employed (managerial economies). Money can be borrowed at competitive rates (financial economies).

Methods of production (page 25)

1 Batch production is using flow production techniques to make different batches of a similar kind of product. When one batch is finished, production switches to a second style.

2 A clothing manufacturer wants to make basic styles so machinery would cut costs. Different styles, finishes and fabrics may be used in batches so that different kinds of customers can be targeted while still using one factory. Workers with basic skills in cutting fabric can be used and they stay motivated because they have different styles to work on.

Efficiency and new technology (page 27)

1 **a)** Automation means a production process entirely managed by machinery.

b) CAM is when computers aid the production process but workers are still involved.

c) Computer control systems use technology to manage part of the production process, in particular, to turn other machines on and off or to keep track of where items are on a production line.

2 Computers could be used to regulate temperatures or to open windows automatically, to control watering systems and to keep track of the different plants stocked in the hothouses.

3 Capital-intensive businesses have a greater part of their production run by machines than people. More money is invested in machinery than is spent on people's wages.

4 Beau employees might find that new technology could save time and effort if lots of small chores could be done automatically. Workers could then spend more time on the more interesting activities. They might have to be retrained, both to manage the technology and in new jobs. There is also a risk that fewer workers will be needed and some might be made redundant.

Quality management (page 29)

1 This could save GRC money by putting the packaging closer to the products. There would be less movement and a manager could keep an eye on the whole process. They could sell the spare site and probably save on some labour costs.

2 **a)** Quality control means checking the quality of the product and the production process to ensure standards are maintained.

b) A high standard of quality control could be obtained by employing inspectors to check the kitchen products at different stages in the production process and ensuring that the best quality materials are used. They could also spend time training staff to the highest level of skills. Alternatively, they could train all workers to operate as teams to check on quality throughout the process. Many eyes are more likely to spot problems before they become too serious.

Business finance (page 31)

1 Internal: retained profit, owners' capital, share sales

   External: bank loan, lease arrangements, grants

2 Restaurant owners may not have enough income to pay for a new restaurant. They may need to use their own cash for other purposes.

Break even (page 33)

1 Fixed cost: sandwich-making equipment; Variable cost: bread.

2 Break even is when revenue just covers costs; 1000/(2–1) = 1000 sandwiches.

3 a) Break-even point = 1000/(1.50–1) = 2000 sandwiches. The break-even level doubles.

   b) Break-even point = 1000/(2–0.60) = 1000/1.4 = 715 sandwiches. The break-even level falls.

   c) Break-even point = 1200/(2–1) = 1200 sandwiches. The break-even level rises.

Cash flow (page 35)

1 It shows likely flows of income and expenditure for the year ahead.

2 Actual cash flow may show variations in the amount of both income and expenditure. It is likely that the net cash flow will be different from the forecast.

3 Fuzz might be short of cash at certain times of the year, especially prior to Christmas.

4 Fuzz might take a short-term loan in the months before Christmas, or they might try to cut costs.

Financial statements (page 37)

1 Could look at the working capital (current assets – liabilities) to see how much funding is available for debt repayment.

2 Expansion plans should be based on a healthy cash flow, a decent and regular profit, a healthy amount of retained profit, and a low interest rate if they intend to borrow money.

Financial performance (page 39)

1 Current ratio = current assets : current liabilities = 4000:800 = 5:1.

2 The company has a healthy asset position and could afford to use some of these assets to expand the business.

People in business (page 41)

1 Workers are poorly motivated because they are not well paid and do not enjoy their jobs.

2 Raise basic pay because it would give them more encouragement to stay on and work hard. Give some additional training – this would give more purpose and responsibility to workers.

Motivation and pay (page 43)

1 a) Cleaner: payment by results and a good basic wage because the job is very satisfying

   b) Salesperson: commission so it encourages him or her to work faster or push a deal more effectively

   c) Nurse: basic salary because results are hard to quantify

   d) Shop assistant: time rate with bonuses because the job is relatively unskilled and you want the worker to make good use of time

   e) Lorry driver: basic wage with opportunity for overtime. You don't want a system which encourages the driver to work flat out because this could be dangerous, but probably need overtime because the time to complete a job can be unpredictable.

2 Financial rewards would help, but she would need to be given responsibility and challenge to make the work interesting.

Recruitment (page 45)

The job description gives a clear vision of the job expectations and can be used later to check the progress of the appointed person. Interviews give both interviewer and candidate an opportunity to meet and decide if they'll get on successfully. This is particularly important in terms of a small business where people have to work closely together with a lot of trust.

Recruitment case study (page 47)

1 Karen because she offers better GCSE grades, some post-16 study, has a reliable, if limited, work experience and an interest in computers

2 What are your strengths? And areas for development?

   How well do you get on with people?

   What do you know about computers?

   Why are you applying for this post?

   What training do you think you will need?

   Where do you see yourself in five years time?

   (These questions will find out about attitude, experience, self-awareness and ambition.)

3 Internal recruitment means finding someone from within the current employees. This can save a lot of time and money, you know the strengths of the person and they know your business.

Training staff (page 49)

1 Limited finance is available to pay for other kinds of training; each small business is likely to have its own way of working, so the new employee needs to train alongside experienced staff.

2 The company might not have the expertise or the spare managers/supervisors to do the training internally. Outside trainers may be more up to date.

Communication at work (page 51)

1 **a)** Employer: advantages – saves office costs, employees are better motivated; disadvantages – lose face-to-face contact, not such close supervision

b) Employee: advantages – can mix home and work life better, added flexibility, cuts travel costs and time; disadvantages – work may be intrusive at home, may incur extra costs (e.g. a printer), can lose personal contact and motivation

2 The business can communicate easily and cheaply with anyone who has Internet access and can deal quickly and directly with customer requests and complaints; customers can research choices of products available quickly, they can order quickly and can send feedback directly to the business.

Industrial relations (page 53)

The employer is breaking the law by not providing written contracts and not following health and safety guidelines. A trade union could negotiate with employers to change the rules, threaten industrial action if the employer won't change and provide information and guidance for workers in making their case.

Negotiating (page 55)

1 **a)** Some orders will be late, but wage costs will be lower.

b) Most production will slow down and some jobs will not get done at all.

c) Orders may be lost, possibly for good if the strike is a long one, but it will save on running costs while the factory is shut.

2 It covers everyone so only one set of negotiations will be needed; there will be no divisions between workers; lines of responsibility will be clearer. If workers need to take action, they will be a more powerful group.

Business and marketing (page 57)

The company could carry out a SWOT analysis. Strengths: which products are the most profitable, which are growing, customer base? Weaknesses: are there any areas where costs are too high or where marketing is poor, do some product lines need to be closed? Opportunities: could the product be sold more easily across Eastern Europe or China, could the firm introduce new products with, say, colour-matched accessories or better text-messaging? Threats: what is the state of potential markets, is there a global slump, what are rival companies doing, how do their prices and product range compare?

Market research (page 59)

1 Typical spending at garages over a period; why they choose a particular petrol station.

2 It would allow the manager to plan a targeted marketing campaign to attract particular kinds of motorist.

The marketing mix (page 61)

1 Large posters for a short period prior to opening, and local leaflets and local newspaper adverts repeated weekly for four weeks prior to opening. This will raise the profile locally and make people aware of the opening. (Costs: five poster sites = £2000; four leaflet sets = £700; four newspaper adverts = £2200)

2 Once the store is open, sustain new interest via young people with competitions at school (prizes £500), meal discounts (1000 at £2 each = £2000), eight radio adverts (twice daily for four days = £2400). Young people can typically be expected to bring along their families. Once eating habits are established, regular 'give-aways' linked to local cinema programmes could be used to sustain interest.

The product life cycle (page 63)

1 A very competitive market is one where lots of rival companies and products are competing for customers. Young people may be able to buy several different shoes with fashionable brands supplied by companies from all over the world. There may be several shoes with very similar prices.

2 Customers may be resistant to a new brand which has no 'street cred'. Allsports may have to spend a large amount of money marketing its brand, for example, having a well-known sports star to champion its product.

Pricing decisions (page 65)

1 Customers might not try the product at all, or if they do, they will not stay with the product unless the distinctive quality is very good.

2 The company might try a loss-leader pricing policy, setting a very low price for another one of their products in order to catch the customers' eyes. Alternatively, they might try price discrimination by selling their product somewhere special, like in train buffets or in airports.

Promoting products (page 67)

Local adverts will attract local custom and that may well be the best source of new customers for Fill-up Foods PLC. It is relatively cheap compared with national advertising but will only reach a limited audience. Local adverts can also be targeted at specific homes via leaflet drops or direct calls on the telephone. The product might be linked into popular local firms.

The business environment (page 69)

The government could help business activity by providing grants for firms that locate in particular places, by cutting taxes for companies, by promoting exports or putting taxes on foreign imports.

Business and competition (page 71)

1 The T-shirt was sold as being fit-for-purpose with faded colour. Unless there is some other fault, the customer is not entitled to her money back (Sale and Supply of Goods Act).

2 Baz could encourage the goodwill of the customer by offering another product in exchange.

3 The customer could get advice from the Citizen's Advice Bureau or the local Trading Standards Office.

4 They could take Baz to the small claims court.

Business and the community (page 73)

1 External benefits might include extra jobs; more spending by workers and visitors to the park; higher profile in the area as a place to visit; the by-pass might be built as part of the development; there might be contributions to a special art feature donated by the park.

2 External costs might include pollution during the development; extra traffic and noise once built; ugly appearance; loss of trade for other leisure attractions in the area.

3 The local council could charge higher business rates, or ask the park to contribute to some other development. The government could tax such developments or ask them to pay a planning fee of some kind. Alternatively, general taxes could be used to cover some of the community costs.

Business ethics (page 75)

1 The Co-op buys food products from suppliers at a fair price to help poorer communities. As a business, it spends money on education projects to fight climate change.

2 More customers might buy products from a business with a good ethical reputation, hence boosting profits. Spending more money on training will help to keep good staff for the future and so cut recruitment costs in the long term.

The national economy (page 77)

1 It means Carco will be able to locate at Kirston with cheaper rates and with local grants to help them.

2 Carco will also benefit from the town's new infrastructure and a ready workforce.

3 Their arrival may encourage other businesses to locate in Kirston and their workers will spend money in the local community. Carco may also purchase products from local businesses. They will eventually pay business rates to the local council.

Business and Europe (page 79)

1 A single market is a shared trading area with common external barriers to protect members and free trading between members within the boundaries.

2 This helps because there are no taxes between the member countries, a common currency makes trade easier and there are common rules about advertising, transport, etc.

3 Firms which set up factories in the EU get grants to help them if they bring employment and are allowed to trade within the EU because their products are made inside the EU boundaries.

The global economy (page 81)

1 a) Japanese visitors will find their yen buys more British pounds. This could encourage more Japanese visitors to come to the craft centre as part of a foreign holiday.

b) Japanese consumers will have less money to spend and may cut back on foreign holidays. This is likely to mean that fewer visitors come to the craft centre.

2 The government could help to keep the exchange rate stable so that Jo's business is not disrupted by unexpected fluctuations. It could also pursue policies which promote lower interest rates so that Jo can expand her business through cheaper loans.

Glossary

A

acid test ratio like current ratio but taking out stocks; a more accurate measure of a business's liquidity

B

balance sheet a record of the value of what a firm owns (its assets), the value of what it owes (its liabilities) and the value of the capital invested in the firm. It is a 'snapshot' taken at a particular point in time (usually the last day of the accounting period).

batch production larger-scale production of 'batches' of similar items

branding developing a product's name with a distinctive logo, colours and packaging, and registering all this to prevent other companies copying it

break even the point at which total revenue equals total costs

business cycle the ups and downs in the level of general business activity in the country

business objectives shows what a business is setting out to achieve in broad terms and as more detailed targets

business plan shows the information and figures which predict the future performance of the business

C

CAD/CAM/CIM use of computers in production to aid or completely manage the process (computer-aided design, computer-aided manufacturing, computer-integrated manufacturing).

cash flow forecast a way of trying to predict what money will come in and what money will go out of a business over a fixed period

chain of command the links in an organisation between people with different roles and responsibilities who take orders and instructions from above and give them to those below.

chain of production businesses which contribute to the complete production process from extraction to final sale

collective bargaining most industries and businesses decide pay and other issues by collective bargaining (negotiating as a group rather than as an individual)

competitive business environment the environment in which a business has to operate, competing against rival businesses in the market

co-operative a business run by a group of people with a shared interest in the business, for the benefit of all involved. Each participant has an equal say.

cost-plus pricing a business adds a percentage mark-up to the total unit costs (variable and fixed) of producing an item

current ratio shows how easily a firm's short-term debts could be paid from current assets

customer-led business which bases its production on market research and customer views

CV (curriculum vitae) written by a job applicant. It lists their qualifications, interests and experience.

D

deed of partnership a set of rules to follow if trust between partners breaks down

desk research working with published material

E

economies of scale reductions in unit costs when producing larger quantities

efficient production producing the maximum output at the least possible cost

entrepreneur person who has the skills for and takes the risks of starting up and running a business in return for profit

equal opportunities law law which ensures equal opportunities, especially in employment

Ethical responsibility the duty to do right rather than wrong; this refers to carrying out business in a fair and honest way with regard to the interests of all stakeholders

Euro from 2002, the Euro has become the single currency for the majority of EU member countries

European Union a common trading area for 27 countries with many shared benefits

exchange rate the value of one currency against another

external communication communication between the business and its customers or suppliers

external costs and benefits costs and benefits of business activity which fall on the community and are not covered by normal prices

external finance finance from outside of a business, e.g. bank loans, grants, trade credit

F

field research collecting and analysing information gained first-hand, via interviews and surveys

financial and non-financial incentive monetary and non-monetary rewards to motivate workers

fixed costs costs of production which don't vary with the amount made

flow (or mass) production continuous production of identical items, e.g. newspapers, glass bottles

franchise allows a small trader to use a well-known company's trade name, and allows the well-known company to use the experience of local managers

G

gross profit margin a measure of the profitability of a business for every £1 of sales

H

horizontal integration businesses choose to link activities in one sector with another in the same sector

Human Resource department the department responsible for recruitment, training and industrial relations in a large business

I

income tax tax on income; the more you earn, the more you pay

induction training training given to new employees to teach the basic skills required for the job and to introduce the employee to the business and its expectations

industrial action action taken by workers to try to put pressure on the management to accept their point of view. Such action might involve a strike (all workers stop work), an overtime ban or a work to rule (doing only those specific tasks which are outlined in your contract).

industrial relations the term used to describe the relationship between the workforce and the management of a business

internal communication communication within an organisation which enables people to do their jobs effectively

internal finance finance from within the business's own resources, e.g. share sales, profits

J

job production making of a unique item from start to finish, e.g. a house extension

just-in-time (lean) production an efficient way of producing. Stocks of raw materials, parts and components arrive in just the right quantity just in time to be used in the production process.

L

limited liability responsibility for the debts of a business is limited to the amount of shares of each owner

loss-leaders a policy which sets prices at or below cost (with no mark-up) in order to penetrate a new market

M

market segments businesses divide customers into different groups, or market segments, according to different characteristics

marketing mix made up of elements of Product, Promotion, Price and Place

Maslow's hierarchy a model of human needs based on a pyramid; basic needs of survival are at the bottom

O

off-the-job training specialist training which involves employees stopping their usual work

on-the-job training training given whilst employees are working

organisation chart shows how a business is divided up by function, by product or by place

P

partnerships businesses owned by the partners (there must be a minimum of two and usually a maximum of twenty partners)

performance-related pay a type of 'payment by results', where pay is linked to achievement of targets

person specification drawn up by an employer, it gives a picture of the ideal candidate for a job, and is used to help decide on the most suitable person for that job

price discrimination charging different prices to different people for the same product

primary data information collected first hand, via interviews and surveys

primary sector businesses involved in getting raw materials from the land or sea, e.g. farming

private limited company (Ltd) company owned by shareholders who have limited liability. Shares only available to friends and family

privatisation the sale of public sector organisations to the private sector by selling shares

productivity a measure of the output per person

product-led a business which makes goods first and then thinks how to sell them

product life cycle products have a natural life cycle which begins with their development, moves through a period of growth to maturity and ends with a loss of sales

profit and loss account a record of revenue (money in) and costs (money out) during the past accounting period (usually a year)

public limited company (PLC) company owned by shareholders who have limited liability. Shares available to the general public

public sector organisation owned and run by the government for the benefit of everyone. Financed by sales of goods and services and also from taxes

R

Return on Capital Employed (ROCE) how much profit is made for every £1 invested

S

secondary data data such as published accounts, government reports and data from consumer groups.

secondary sector businesses using raw materials to produce finished goods, e.g. a computer manufacturer

shareholders people who have bought shares in a company and are therefore part owners

skimming (or creaming) the market charging a high price for a product while it is fashionable

sole trader a business owned and controlled by one person

span of control the range of responsibility of any manager

stakeholders people who have an interest in the success of a business. Their objectives are often different.

SWOT analysis helps a business to look at its strengths and weaknesses, and the opportunities and threats in the market

T

tertiary sector businesses providing a service to industry or to consumers, e.g. banking

Total Quality Management (TQM) a system of quality management which places responsibility for quality on all employees throughout the production process

trade unions and trade associations represent some workers and employers in discussions and disputes

V

Value Added Tax (VAT) a tax on spending on most goods and services

variable costs business costs which are linked to the amount of goods or services produced

vertical integration businesses choose to link activities in one sector with those in another

W

working capital current assets – current liabilities: a measure of a business's ability to meet immediate payments

Last-minute learner

- **These four pages give you the most important facts across the whole subject in the smallest possible space.**
- **You can use these pages as a final check.**
- **You can also use them as you revise as a way to check your learning.**
- **You can cut them out for quick and easy reference.**

Business types and objectives
Businesses can be classified by sectors, by type and by their different objectives.

Sectors of business activity
- **Primary** sector (extraction, e.g. farming).
- **Secondary** sector (manufacturing, e.g. car company).
- **Tertiary** sector (services, e.g. banking).

Businesses may integrate (link) their production activities, vertically (across sectors) or horizontally (in same sector).

Different types of business
- **Sole traders**: owned and controlled by one person.
- **Partnerships**: owned by 2–20 partners.
- **Companies**: private limited companies (Ltds) and public limited companies (PLCs). The 'limited' refers to limited liability. Shareholders are the owners, have a say in running the company and share in its profits.
- **Co-operatives**: run by people with a shared business interest, to benefit all involved. Each participant has an equal say.
- **Franchises**: allows a trader to use a well-known company's trade name and enables the company to benefit from the experience of local managers.

- **Public sector organisations**: owned and controlled by the government. Financed by taxes as well as by selling goods and services.

Business organisation
In a small business, the owner has responsibility for major decisions and so communications can be direct with everyone involved. Larger businesses need a structure and more formal communication. Decisions can be hard to manage with long chains of command or large spans of control.

A large business my be divided up by:
- **function** (e.g. marketing, finance)
- **product** (e.g. Ford vans and cars)
- **geographical area** (e.g. Ford UK, Ford Spain).

Business objectives
Businesses may aim to make a profit, to provide a service or to be charitable.

Stakeholders' objectives are often different:
- customers: value for money, choice
- owners: survival in business, best return on investment
- managers: best salary, status for department
- local community: local jobs, clean environment
- suppliers: repeat orders, reliable payment of bills
- employees: job satisfaction, good pay.

Business production
- Business production involves the use of **raw materials**, **labour** and **capital/investment** with an entrepreneur to take the risks.
- Production can be product-led or customer-led.
- Different businesses may produce a single product, a wide product range or a wide product mix.
- Larger firms can take advantage of **economies of scale** (reductions in unit costs when producing larger quantities). Economies of scale may be:
  - **technical** – using machinery more effectively
  - **trading** – buy in bulk
  - **financial** – borrow more at lower rates of interest
  - **managerial** – use highly-skilled management.
- There are three production methods, each with its own advantages and disadvantages:

	Advantages	Disadvantages
Job production	High quality product Job satisfaction high	Expensive materials and labour Slow process
Batch production	Lower unit costs More specialised machinery	Costly storage and movement Some repetition in jobs Machinery needs resetting
Flow production	Large output, low unit cost Good use of production time Low-skilled, easily-trained labour Products of standard quality	Large investment in machinery Inflexible Breakdowns expensive Boring work

- **Business efficiency** (maximum output at the least possible cost) can be measured by:
  - productivity (e.g. output per person)
  - unit costs (total costs divided by quantity produced)
  - other measures (e.g. stock levels, product quality).
- **Just-in-time** (or lean) production is an efficient way of producing if carefully managed:
  - parts in just the right quantity, just in time to be used, saving time and money
  - computer-controlled information links are vital
  - breakdowns in the system can be costly.
- Use of **computers** in **business production** can cut labour costs but requires big investment:
  - CAM (computer-aided manufacturing)
  - CAD (computer-aided design)
  - CIM (computer-integrated manufacturing).

There are various methods of **quality control**:
- sample checks by specialists
- research and development departments (develop new products)
- total quality management (responsibility for quality on all employees, e.g. Japanese idea of continual improvement (Kaizen); workers suggest improvements wherever possible).
- **Factors affecting business location**:
  - labour (e.g. need for a highly skilled workforce)
  - raw materials and the market (e.g. be near to where goods are produced or sold)
  - land (e.g. amount and cost of land, planning restrictions)
  - infrastructure and services (e.g. good communications and transport links)
  - UK and European governments' financial support (e.g. tax-free grants and subsidies).

Business finance
- Finance is essential to pay for:
  - start-up costs
  - regular running costs
  - unexpected events
  - investment.
- The **finance** for a business can come from:
  - inside (**internal finance**) via owners' funds, share sales, retained profits
  - outside the business (**external finance**) through loans, grants, trade credit, leasing.
- Good financial management requires a good **business plan**, estimates of **break-even** (where revenue just covers costs) and charging a **reasonable price** for a product.
- A price must be enough to cover fixed and variable costs as well as making a profit.
- Regular **cash flow forecasts** and budgets predict money in and out over a fixed period. A profitable firm, without enough cash to pay its **creditors**, may have to cease trading.
- **Detailed accounts** help managers to judge the success of business activities:

1 Profit and loss account
- A record of revenue (money in) and costs (money out) during the past accounting period (usually a year).
- Different parts of the account are used by different groups to judge progress.
- The trading account shows gross profit (sales revenue – cost of sales).
- Government uses the net profit figure to decide how much tax should be paid.
- Lenders and shareholders use the dividend figure to judge the business's success and to assess how risky it is to invest further.

2 Balance sheet
- A record of the value of what a firm owns (assets), what it owes (liabilities) and the capital invested in the firm. It is a 'snapshot' taken at a particular point in time (usually last day of the accounting period):
- Assets = fixed assets + current assets (stock + debtors + cash)
- Liabilities = short-term liabilities + long term liabilities
- Working capital = current assets – current liabilities
- Capital & reserves = share capital + retained profit.
- Accountants ensure that the figure for 'where the money is' (assets – liabilities) is equal to 'where the money came from' (capital & reserves).

3 Performance ratios

Ratio	What does it show?	Who might be interested?
Profitability		
Gross profit margin Gross profit : sales revenue $\frac{\text{Gross profit}}{\text{Sales revenue}} \times 100\%$	Gross profit for every £1 of sales. The bigger the %, the greater the profit.	Managers – is the firm performing well? Creditors – are profits enough to repay loans?
Net profit margin Net profit : sales revenue $\frac{\text{Net profit}}{\text{Sales revenue}} \times 100\%$	As before, but now allowing for fixed costs.	As above.
Return on capital employed (ROCE) Net profit : capital employed $\frac{\text{Net profit}}{\text{Capital employed}} \times 100\%$	Profit created from each £1 invested.	Shareholders (investors) – is investment providing as good a return as other options might?
Liquidity		
Current ratio Current assets : current liabilities	How easily a firm's short-term debts could be paid from current assets. Ratio of 1 : 1 means a firm is just covering its debts.	Managers, creditors – how easily can the firm's debts be covered?
Acid test ratio current assets – stock : current liabilities	Removes stocks from the equation, to give a more realistic measure. A reasonable figure is seen as between 0.5 : 1 and 1 : 1.	As above.

People in business

- **Recruitment and training** are organised by:
  - the manager (small business)
  - the Human Resource department (large business).
- Motivation theories help to explain people's behaviour:
  - **Maslow's** Hierarchy ranks people's needs in order of importance. Basic needs must always be met but, in the long term, workers need to feel fulfilled, possibly by being given responsibilities.
- **Financial incentives** (e.g. good wages, fringe benefits) and **non-financial incentives** (e.g. varied work, praise, promotion) affect people's motivation. Different types of payment include:
  - wages and salaries/overtime
  - bonus payments
  - performance-related pay.
- A typical company **recruitment process** includes: a job description; a job advertisement; interviews with candidates; checking references; providing a contract and training.
- Training is vital to a business's success. **Properly trained staff**:
  - are more productive
  - stay longer with a business
  - are more likely to obtain promotion.
- **Induction training** teaches the skills required for a job and introduces the rules of a business.
- **Government training** improves workers' qualifications and helps unemployed people.

- **Good communication** helps people do their jobs effectively. There are several types of communication:
  - internal: between employees in the business
  - external: between the business and its customers
  - written: provides a permanent record (e.g. memos, emails, reports)
  - verbal: quick and direct (meetings, telephone calls, conversations).
  Many routine tasks can now be done more quickly and easily using ICT.
- **Good industrial relations** are vital:
  - Trade Unions speak for workers; Trade Associations speak for employers.
  - Most industries and businesses decide pay and other issues by collective bargaining.
  - Industrial action (e.g. strikes, working to rule) is difficult and costly but necessary at times.
  - There are laws covering **working conditions**, including equal opportunities and a safe workplace:

Things an employer must do	Things an employer must not do
Provide a written statement on conditions, e.g. pay	Discriminate against workers on grounds of race, age, gender or disability
Give equal pay to men and women if they are doing the same work	Stop a worker from belonging to a trade union
Give specific benefits to workers who have completed two years with the firm	Employ children under 13
Follow health and safety laws	Dismiss a worker unfairly

Business and marketing

- **SWOT analysis** (**S**trengths, **W**eaknesses, **O**pportunities, **T**hreats) helps a business to plan for the future.
- Businesses use **research** to help develop marketing strategies.
  - Customers are split into market **segments** by income, education and occupation.
  - Focus groups (based on gender, age, race, etc.) can be asked their opinion of a product.
  - **Desk research** is conducted using **secondary data**; **field research** involves collecting **primary data**.
- There are different **types of survey**: one-on-one questionnaires; postal surveys; random surveys; surveys based on quotas.
- **Survey questions** can be either **closed** (easy to analyse, but provides limited data) or open (provides more information, but harder to analyse).
- **The marketing mix**: 'four Ps':
  Product, **P**romotion, **P**rice and **P**lace.
  - Different companies emphasise different elements of the marketing mix.
  1 **Product**: e.g. quality, range, after-sales service, features and facilities, size and packaging
  2 **Price**: e.g. basic price level, discounts, different pricing for different customer segments

  3 **Promotion** (vital at product launch): e.g. how much expenditure, style and substance, timing, media
  4 **Place**: e.g. what distribution chain to use, direct selling, delivery and stock levels
- Products have a natural **life cycle**: development and launch; growth to maturity; market is full of similar products; loss of sales; end of cycle.
- The **product development** process involves: establishing customer needs; generating new ideas; checking production is possible; testing prototypes; developing a marketing strategy.
- **Product life cycles** can be lengthened by: extra advertising and promotion; new packaging; special deals; widening the product range; changing the product image; diversifying a product.
- **Branding** involves developing a distinctive name and logo, colours and packaging.
- **Prices, supply and demand theory**:
  - The higher the price: the more will be supplied; the less will be demanded.
  - Too low a price: demand will outstrip supply.
  - Too high a price: there will be a surplus of unsold products.
  - The equilibrium price will satisfy both a business and its customers.

- Pricing policies are used to persuade customers to buy a product:
  - cost-plus pricing (a percentage mark-up)
  - competitive pricing (price like competitors')
  - loss-leaders (prices below cost to penetrate a new market)
  - skimming the market (high price while in fashion)
  - price discrimination (charging different prices to different people for the same product).

- Most companies advertise through a variety of media: TV, radio and cinema; newspapers and magazines; journals or specialist publications; posters.
- Sales promotion activities include: special offers; price discounts; vouchers, coupons and customer loyalty cards; joint promotions; point of sale materials; free gift campaigns or prize competitions.

The business environment

- Competition can be good because:
  - it keeps businesses on their toes
  - it gives consumers a choice of products.
- Competition may be bad if:
  - businesses make exaggerated claims for their products
  - a firm dominates the market, ignoring customer views
  - some undesirable products are made for profit (e.g. cigarettes, alcohol).
- The three main laws protecting the consumer are:
  - Trade Descriptions Act (1968 and 1972): stops businesses giving misleading information.
  - Consumer Credit Act 1974: protection when borrowing or buying on credit.
  - Sale and Supply of Goods Act 1994: products have to be of 'satisfactory quality'.
- The external business environment is full of risks:
  - The ups and downs in the economy can make it hard to sell a new product.
  - An unforeseen problem with a product may be found.
  - Rivals may use technology to make a better product.
  - Interest rates may rise, increasing the cost of loans.
  - Exchange rates may change, making foreign trade more difficult.

- **The government** manages the economy to provide stability for businesses and ensure everyone benefits from business activity:
  - It taxes income, spending and business profits.
  - It uses the money for welfare benefits, services like health and education, and investment in new roads and buildings.
  - It aims to support poorer regions of the country, e.g. grants to encourage businesses to locate within a designated area.
- UK businesses operate in a **European Union** shared by 27 countries with a market of some 500 million people:
  - EU rules help and control business activity.
  - Over 58% of the UK's overseas trade is with other EU countries.
  - The EU is financed by contributions from member states and tariffs on imports from outside the EU.
  - EU membership may continue to expand as further European countries join.
  - The Euro is a common currency used by most EU members but not currently the UK.

Notes

Notes